Let's face it, most PhD dissertations are audience. This is especially true for those on theological or biblical themes. Thankfully, Ian Darke offers a lifeline! This book provides clear, practical examples of transforming complex dissertations into engaging resources for the everyday Christian reader. If you've ever dreamt of sharing your research with a wider audience, this is the guide you've been waiting for.

Milton Acosta, Associate Director of Global Training, United World Mission

One of the quiet tragedies among theological educators in the Global South takes the form of unpublished doctoral dissertations lying unpublished and unread on young scholars' shelves. The fruit of blood, sweat, and tears, these book-length works are evidence that an emerging scholar has cut the mustard and proven himself or herself capable of the scholarly vocation. Yet the dissertation is not and cannot be a product that a waiting public can 'take up and read', to quote Augustine's well-known anecdote. Before it can become useful in this second way and for this wider public, the doctoral dissertation requires a transformation that is too often unrealized amid the hurly-burly of academic life and service.

The loss is incalculable.

Ian Darke, better placed than anyone I know to address this issue, has produced a kind of shepherd's manual intended to lead a dispersed doctoral flock across the plains and through the valleys that lie between the graduated 'doctor' and the publishing of his doctoral labours as a fresh, accessible, and well-tuned gift to the reading public.

Darke knows better than to suggest that the dissertation-to-book transformation will be easy. It is in fact his realism about the task that makes him the expert guide.

Here's hoping that a modest army of dusty doctoral dissertations will be rescued from obscurity and converted into the treasured and digestible volumes we need to read. Here's hoping that the Augustinian 'take up and read' will in consequence bear fresh and abundant fruit.

David A Baer, Director, Theological Education Initiative and Professor of Old Testament and Biblical Languages, Biblical Seminary of Colombia

The publishing landscape can be opaque to outsiders and non-experts. For the recent graduate weighing what to do with a hard-earned completed thesis – how best to make it serve a career and a public in need of its findings – there are many factors to consider. This book takes the mystery out of the process for those with something to say about Christianity, in particular. Ian Darke has pulled back the curtain on how publishers across the globe, and Christian publishers in particular, think about your thesis and has given us a wonderful book of specific, practical, detailed advice for revising your work and placing it where it belongs in the current landscape.

Dr Stephanie L Derrick is a Los Angeles based screenwriter and an award-winning historian of religion in the modern era. She did her PhD in History at the University of Stirling (Scotland).

From Dissertation to Christian Book is a helpful guide for any academic looking to shape their scholarship in such a way that it appeals to a broader audience. This distillation of tools, tips, and practices will serve students and professors alike as they craft their writing to communicate to the church and the world.

Rachel Hastings, academic editor

The task of mining and searching scripture for answers to contemporary and contextual issues lies largely on the shoulders of Bible scholars. So much study and research and thought and prayer goes into so many dissertations. If this content is not re-expressed for a wider audience, it risks remaining trapped in an academic echo chamber.

Ian Darke, writing from decades of experience with local publishers and writers, and with a heart for relevant, life changing literature, shows how that gap can be bridged and the impacts multiplied. This is a valuable and hugely practical resource. It should be on the mandatory reading list, not just for all those scholars who have been called to write, but also for Majority World editors and publishers everywhere.

Colin J Macpherson, Director of Publisher Development, Langham Partnership International

Let us hope that Ian Darke's *From Dissertation to Christian Book* becomes required reading at Bible colleges and seminaries around the world. Imagine the wealth of published materials that would result, as emerging leaders catch the vision for repurposing the same valuable insights found in their scholarly writing for a more popular audience. Darke motivates his readers to be good stewards of their learning and words, not limiting themselves to a small audience of academics but serving the wider church, both local and global. He also gives clear, practical guidance to first-time authors regarding the publishing process – seasoned tips gained from his decades in publishing ministry in Latin America. This book meets a strategic need and does the global Church a great service.

John Maust, President, Media Associates International

From Dissertation to Christian Book is a short book full of wise and practical advice that has been tried and tested. I will be recommending it to our authors and to those who send us proposals that are in need of further development.

Sam Richardson, CEO, SPCK Group

REGNUM PRACTITIONER SERIES

FROM DISSERTATION TO CHRISTIAN BOOK

REGNUM PRACTITIONER SERIES PREFACE

While we delight to serve the academic community, our mission is to enable the global church to engage more readily in God's mission in its very diverse contexts. To do this we seek to bring practitioners and academics together. Our desire is that this series will bridge the gap that sometimes exists between, on the one hand, Christian leaders and mission practitioners and, on the other, Christian researchers.

About the Author

Ian Darke studied Pure Mathematics at the universities of London and Warwick. After serving for a few years in the UCCF (Universities and Colleges Christian Fellowship) he was invited to work with the equivalent student ministry in Peru (AGEUP), where he also taught mathematics at the Universidad Nacional Mayor de San Marcos in Lima. Since 1990 Ian has been dedicated to the development of publishing houses in Latin America. He was a co-founder of Ediciones Puma in Peru, works with Ediciones Certeza Unida (IVP in Spanish) and coordinates the Letra Viva network of evangelical publishing ministries in Latin America. He was the coordinator of the Latin America Bible commentary project (*Comentario bíblico contemporáneo*). He and his wife live in San José, Costa Rica. They have two children and three granddaughters. He is a keen runner.

FROM DISSERTATION TO CHRISTIAN BOOK

A Guide on Using a Thesis to Produce a Readable Publication

Ian Darke

First published 2024 by Regnum Books International
Regnum is an imprint of the Oxford Centre for Mission Studies
St. Philip and St. James Church, Woodstock Road, Oxford, OX2 6HR, UK
www.regnumbooks.net

British Library Cataloguing in Publication Data
A catalogue record for this book is available from the British Library

ISBN: 979-8-8898-3863-0
eBook ISBN: 979-8-8898-3864-7

Typeset in Palatino by WORDS BY DESIGN

regnum

Distributed by Fortress Press in the US, Canada, India, and Brazil

Contents

From Dissertation to Christian Book

PREFACE

During our years working in Latin America, we have had contact with many Christian scholars who have studied abroad for a doctorate or a master's degree and who then want to publish their dissertation. In many cases, after contacting an editorial company, the crestfallen scholar hears that his or her work would be impossible to publish in its original form of a thesis.

At the same time, many of the Christian publishers I work with in the Letra Viva publishing network long to produce new books in Spanish that are relevant, contextualised and biblical. Often the publisher doesn't have the time or experience to work with a scholar to 'mine' a dissertation and so produce material of benefit to the church. All too often both the scholar and the publisher end up with disappointment and frustration.

This problem is not limited to Latin America, as in other regions of the world the same story is told. The situation can be particularly acute for those scholars from the Majority World who have spent years in residential study at a North American or European institution and who on returning 'home' are readjusting to Global South life and ministry. With feelings of dislocation and relocation, it can seem challenging to connect elegant but rarified doctoral work with the messy and confusing world of ordinary ministry.

One solution could be to provide the scholars themselves with the tools to adapt their dissertation or to extract from it material that will be of wide benefit. The opportunity to show fruit from their studies in an accessible, published form should be a helpful step for the scholar in bridging the worlds of study and service, providing material to help the church grow in depth and also enabling the scholar to develop in their Christian service.

In what follows, by 'dissertation' we do not only mean a doctoral thesis, but also any written work produced from a guided academic study. In this context, the word 'book' we use as a shorthand to mean not only fine-looking hardbacks but also paperbacks, booklets, magazine articles, journal entries, blogs and web documents. In other words, any possible means by which the written word is used to communicate truth to a wider audience.

This small book consists of a compilation of ideas and recommendations from many sources: from manuals written by major university presses aimed at helping doctoral students to work in academia; friends involved in theological education around the world; colleagues in Christian publishing ministries; as well as both cryptic and hilarious e-mails sent by friends.

I express my deep thanks to all my friends who have contributed ideas to this work, and to God our Father, our Lord Jesus, the Word Incarnate and the Spirit who moves hearts.

Ian Darke
March 2024

1. Writing is Important

The short chapters that follow aim to help you answer questions such as: **What** is the key message you have to communicate? **Who** do you want to touch with that message? **Where** can your book or article be best published? **Why** specifically do you want to publish? Also, **how** in detail can you 'mine' your dissertation to produce a book or an article that will serve the church or a community?

Let's start with the exciting thought that through publishing you are connecting to a host of Christian servants throughout the ages. The church has always been 'a people of The Book and books.' The God who 'spoke' and thereby created the cosmos speaks to us through a book of prose and poetry. God inspired the creative genius of narrators and storytellers, historians and poets, prophets and evangelists, who in the pages of a single book have given us God's Word. In our world of immediate and visual communication, it is significant that there is a special place in the Bible given to writing.

Over the centuries the church has understood the importance of the written word, using whatever material or medium was appropriate at that time. Rolls and scrolls gave way to parchment, the hand-printed book, the mass-market paperback, the web page and the e-book. The technology may have changed, but the importance of the written word remains constant: to help readers understand the Bible, to deepen their faith, to relate to the world about them and also to amuse and delight.

The history of the church is full of stories of creative publishing and distribution: of books being copied out by hand by medieval scribes; Luther's tracts produced on the new technology of printing with illustrations by Dürer; the transatlantic trade in sermons by Jonathan Edwards during the Great Revival; 'colporters' carrying books into the mountains of the Andes; and the distribution of books to believers in 'closed countries' in recent times.

THE NEED FOR FRESH PUBLICATIONS

Many books from the past continue in print today – just think of Augustine, Luther, Bunyan and CS Lewis. But there is a need for new books that give fresh insights into faith, that help each Christian respond to the ever-changing culture around them – including challenges thrown up by technology, law, politics and medical ethics – and which communicate with the broader community.

This is especially so for the church in the Majority World. Andrew Walls observes that the centre of gravity of the Christian church has moved 'south.'[1] Because of this shift, the churches in Asia, Africa and Latin America need materials prepared from and for their context. Translated books can be of great service but may also give a distorted and 'foreign' perspective to Christian life and witness. There is an urgent need for books that speak in the language of the people, address the issues of the day and communicate in a culturally appropriate way.

Within each region and continent, there is a particular need for books that not only speak with a local accent, relevant to the peoples of each country, but are also profoundly biblical. While distortions and parodies of the faith sadly abound, the world needs good books. Riad Kassis of Langham Ministries writes:

> *John Stott once said that 'we should be BBC Christians', espousing Balanced Biblical Christianity. Fulfilling the Great Commission, to his mind, required deep theological foundations and, more importantly, the equipping of pastors, evangelists and 'ordinary' Christians to create disciples in whatever situation they are in. The question is, what can we do to encourage our church leaders and preachers to increase their understanding of the Bible, and use it to inspire our churches to make real impacts in our communities?*

In many parts of the world, residential theological education is not an option. But books have the advantage of being able to reach church leaders and preachers, wherever they are, and with relatively modest costs, and be agents for change for the good.

---

[1] Andrew Walls, 'Vulnerable, Interacting, Incarnate Faith,' *The Gospel and Our Culture Newsletter* 26 (1999).

PUBLICATIONS THAT CONNECT

It is interesting to compare the process of publishing with that of the preacher. Charles Spurgeon, sometimes called the 'Prince of Preachers,' was famed for his ability to speak with a direct appeal to the people. In 1898 Walter Thornbury described a visit to Surrey Music Hall to hear him preach:

> *a congregation consisting of 10,000 souls, streaming into the hall, mounting the galleries, humming, buzzing, and swarming – a mighty hive of bees… After waiting for more than half an hour… Mr Spurgeon ascended his tribune… the preacher held us fast-bound for about two hours… It is enough to say of his voice, that its power and volume are sufficient to reach everyone in that vast assembly; of his language that it is neither high-flown nor homely; of his style, that it is at times familiar, at times declamatory, but always happy, and often eloquent…*[2]

Spurgeon had gifts of communication in abundance. Without microphones, he could make himself heard, captivating his congregation with a message that was clear, eloquent and declared with conviction. Maidservants and society ladies alike came to listen, their hearts and minds eager to be affected. They left as changed people.

Just as it would be odd for an evangelist or preacher to feel satisfied to preach to an empty room, similarly, the purpose of publishing a book is that it should be read and that lives will be transformed. A book is not a sermon. But, like a sermon no one hears, a book is not fulfilling its potential if it is never read. Books don't sell themselves, especially in the present culture, with so many voices shouting to be heard. So we need to think through how to give our books the Spurgeon touch.

As we have seen, Charles Spurgeon was known as the Prince of Preachers and drew huge crowds to hear him. Less well known is that he also had a great impact through the published word. Of course, in his day there was no recording technology, and Spurgeon

---

[2] Walter Thornbury, *Old and New London: A Narrative of its History, its People, and its Places* (London: Cassell and Co., 1898).

did not preach from a prepared text but extemporised from notes prepared the evening before. It was arranged for a team of stenographers to sit in the front row to transcribe the messages. These were collated, checked, typeset, printed and distributed all within the week, not through formal bookstores but rather via a network of grocery shops, butchers and newsagents. Between 1855 and 1892, sermons were printed weekly with a readership of approximately 50,000 for each issue!

Wherever you come from, and wherever you are based, you have the opportunity to stand in a glorious lineage of men and women who have contributed to the growth of God's Kingdom through the publication of materials that are fresh, relevant, connect with readers and which reach the people who need them.

2. MESSAGE

The first three fundamental questions to ask of a dissertation are:

- What is the *core message* of your thesis that you want to communicate?
- *Who* do you want to reach with that message
- *Who* can you *feasibly* reach?

These aspects, of 'message' and 'market,' are interconnected. It is hard to think of one without the other. What is the key idea of your dissertation? What would be helpful or of interest to a reader? What is there in your thesis that is novel or useful? Here are some ways that might help you clarify your message:

PINPOINTING A CONVERSATION

In a conference for editors, and reflecting on the role of books in culture, the Mexican writer Gabriel Zaid wrote that the art of publishing lies in identifying an ongoing 'conversation' between thinkers or readers and then publishing a book that will stoke the fires of that debate.[1]

Following this analogy, can you identify who is talking, thinking, arguing or reading about your subject? And then can you see how some elements of your dissertation can add to that discussion? The idea is that the book will be part of a debate, so it will be important to link in some way with the ongoing discussion, to be aware of what has gone before, what are the issues in the air and where the conversation might travel in the future.

Maybe your area of expertise is of interest to scholars who debate the dating of the Book of Daniel, or those interested in Christian responses to the ecological crisis or who are concerned about the relations between church and state. Does your dissertation have

---

[1] Gabriel Zaid, in Jorge Herralde (ed.), *Mito o realidad del libro* (Colombia: CERLALC, 1994). My translation.

something fresh and relevant that will be added to an ongoing conversation?

It may be that your dissertation doesn't offer anything particularly new, but rather provides a clear overview of a contemporary debate which will illuminate the discussion for a general readership. While there is no point in duplicating what has already been said, there could be value in explaining the issues at stake to a wider or even to a different audience. Successful books have been published on the different perspectives that Christians hold on issues in bioethics, intelligent design, creation and evolution, psychology and animal rights.

Some seemingly technical subjects may have deep pastoral consequences, which cry out for explanation. For example, many have concerns about *in vitro* fertilisation which affects them or their loved ones deeply.

Gabriel Zaid suggests that if you can't spot an ongoing debate, maybe it would be the time to form a club of interested parties, to raise the issue and to find people who could be as fascinated with the subject as you are. Your research might have highlighted what the Bible says about including people with disabilities in the church, or the concept of adoption related to family life, or brought to light a fresh way of reading the Book of Esther. Where can you find people interested in your key concerns?

Consideration of a particular 'conversation' your work could feed into will also give you a pointer to the How or Where of publishing the book. If the key works of the debate have all been published by the University of Chattanooga Press, maybe it would be worth looking at publishing with them. If your focus is on issues in Bolivian jurisprudence, make sure it is published in that country.

SHOWCASING ONE CORE IDEA

Experienced academic editor Laura Portwood-Stacer writes of the importance of identifying one core thesis in your work. [2] Many dissertations contain a mish-mash of ideas which could be

[2] Laura Portwood-Stacer, *The Book Proposal Book: A Guide for Scholarly Authors* (Princeton, USA: Princeton University Press, 2021).

suggestive and fruitful in an academic thesis but which would be less useful in a published book. You need to focus on one clear lesson or idea. As Portwood-Stacer says, strong arguments make for strong books and this one core idea is what will drive everything. It will drive the writing style, the sequence of chapters that will be included, a potential title and the way the published book will be promoted!

Portwood-Stacer writes for PhD students from major universities who are aiming to convert their dissertation into a book that will help them launch successful academic careers in a secular setting. Interestingly, her tips on finding that core have an almost evangelical feel:

- 'Is there *one change in the world* that you hope your book will achieve?' Identify it then focus on it with passion and single-mindedness. A core idea from a thesis on the theology of disability might be to show, from a biblical perspective, that the church should reach out and include people with a disability. Then write the book with conviction and passion.
- 'Is there one thing in your thesis that will change minds?' Some Christians feel that climate change is a matter that doesn't concern them. Your core point could be to convince readers they should develop a concern for the environment. Write with clarity and persuasiveness.
- 'Is there one lesson that a reader will take away?' Based on a dissertation on hymns, spiritual songs and singing in the Early Church, you might want to impress upon the reader that Ephesians 5.19 and Colossians 3.16 suggest that we should all take singing more seriously!
- One other suggestion she makes is more personal: 'What most changed *my* thinking as a result of this research?' In some social sciences, it is appropriate to acknowledge the viewpoint of the writer, but most academic writing is cool. Your feelings or personal thoughts are irrelevant. However, these could become a powerful starting point for a book.

A good practice would be to write down, in just one sentence, the core idea that you want to communicate. Avoid the jargon of thesis writing. Avoid deadly red-flag phrases such as: 'I argue that,' 'I examine' and 'an exploration of the concepts.' Leaving these in place is a guaranteed way for a publisher to reject your book idea!

Having written down this core idea, you can then go on to write, in a paragraph, a little more of the content of the book: the key theme or message, the major points and the format or structure that you will follow. Then expand the book idea into something concrete. At this point, you will have travelled a long way towards your goal.

WHAT'S NEW?

Whether you aim to produce a book for a general audience or academia, relating to an ongoing conversation or showcasing one key idea, it is important to ask: Are there books already available in this field that cover the same ground? And what will your book offer that is unique?

Investigate the books published in your subject. You could start by searching with online retailers like Amazon, but also specialist booksellers with an online presence, such as Blackwell's. During your research, you will have already accessed a university library for academic resources, but it would be worth going back with a wider remit according to the breadth of ideas you will cover.

In the case of specific specialised areas, it would be good to listen on the grapevine if a similar book is *about* to be published!

If the only books on your subject have been directed at an academic public, and you aim to reach a wide audience, then you would be well placed to produce a book that popularises important ideas, as we discussed above.

This would be a good moment to share the results of your thesis, your 'book idea' and your initial ideas on how to share it, with a range of people and in a variety of places. As you explain the key ideas of your work and respond to questions, you will learn a lot about both how to refine the core message of your thesis and the potential 'market' for the book to be published.

This process can be tough after years of deep involvement in your research. Some scholars have reported feeling depressed, overwhelmed or diminished as a person as they start their journey towards publication. Be kind to yourself. It can help to take a break and come back to the dissertation with fresh eyes. Talking over the project with wise colleagues or advisors can help. Be encouraged that Christian people are interested in ideas that are relevant to them, in learning something new and growing in their faith and understanding.

3. Market or Readership

The very meaning of 'publishing' is to 'make public' a message. Book publishers all agree that one thing you cannot do is to publish a book that will interest 'everyone.' 'Everyone' is No one. The danger of being vague about who the book is for can lead to it being ignored by 'everyone.'

Once you are clear about the core message of your book, the next questions are: Who will benefit from reading it? Who will be interested in reading it? Who are your potential readers?

Your Readership or 'Market'

We have friends in West Africa who produce materials in an indigenous language which they sell at a book table in (literally) a local market. Before setting off, they think carefully about which books to take, as each local market is different, and which books will be of most interest. They also have to think about how to create shade so that passersby can stop and talk comfortably, as well as what to do if there is a sudden downpour! Few of us will have the experience of taking our books to an open-air market. But you could try imagining yourself at a village market stall, drawing in passersby in the hope that they will buy your book!

Think carefully – just like our friends in West Africa – about your potential readers, *where* will they come across the book, *how* they will respond to it and *what* will motivate them to buy and read it.

Publishers often talk about the 'market' for a book, by which they simply mean the group of people we want to reach. Identifying those potential readers, their interests, habits and the places they might buy books, are key factors in deciding how and where your book should be produced.

Sometimes the potential readers are not the same as the book's potential buyers. Children read books, but books for children will be usually bought by parents, friends or grandparents. So publishers take into account the two 'publics': child readers and adult buyers.

Something similar can arise in other contexts, too. One research project investigated why men were more frequently dropping out of church than women. The research included statistics, interviews and analysis. The author planned then to produce a book for men who had already left church, to encourage them to go back. However, almost by definition, it seemed unlikely that men who had decided to stop going to church would buy a book insisting they should return! Shifting focus, the research provided the basis for a book for pastors who are dealing with that situation. Also a short book, with wise counsel and encouragement, for those wives who were concerned for their wandering husbands.

Be creative and take the opportunity to talk with booksellers and serious readers. Your potential book-buyer will ask themself: 'How will this book help me?' 'Why should I spend good money on this book?'

What are their 'felt needs'? Focus on a key idea that will help real people and make that clear and appealing to potential readers who could be browsing in a bookshop or a market stall.

On Identifying Felt Needs

One characteristic of the Bible commentaries written by theologian John Stott is that they respond to questions asked by his readers. He identified the 'felt needs' of his potential readers receiving input throughout a year as he shared his studies on one Bible book through sermons, seminary classes and study groups. That exposure to all sorts of people enabled him to hear their questions and concerns and also to find out if he was communicating clearly. By the time it came to putting the final text together, he already knew the questions that were commonly raised, and how best to communicate the message.[1]

It would be a mistake to think about your potential public or readership as a 'them,' a group you have identified out there who might be interested in your book, but with whom you have no connection. Colombian theologian Milton Acosta talks about 'finding your niche': looking for those people, in your own country

---

[1] As related in Timothy Dudley-Smith, *John Stott: The Making of a Leader* (Leicester, UK, IVP, 1999).

or elsewhere, with whom you can communicate and establish a relationship.[2] This niche might be local, or indeed national or international.

It is important to ask not only: Do you know your public? But also: Do they know you? Are you active in the circles that are relevant to your research? Do you go to conferences or regular meetings? What other ways can you think of making face-to-face contact with your niche?

Face-to-face contact is ideal. However, though social media may not be everyone's 'cup of tea,' it can be an important way to find your niche, to make your work known and also to hear what your public thinks. The more you can learn about your public, the better you can write for them. This is particularly important if your book is of interest to a wider audience. As Rachel Hastings of InterVarsity Press says:

> *The broader the audience, the deeper the need to establish a meaningful felt need. This can sometimes be challenging with dissertations, as they often meet the felt needs of a very narrow audience, thus requiring a fundamental shift in the approach and structure to broaden the audience of the book.*[3]

CREDIBILITY

If you plan to write about prayer, a publisher will ask: 'What will your book offer that other books on prayer do not offer?' More particularly, what is there in your book about prayer that is missing in books by Philip Yancey, Jim Packer, Don Carson, James Houston, John White or other well-known authors?

Now more than ever, potential readers look to see *who* the author is. When a new book appeared by John Grisham, John le Carré or JK Rowling, thousands went out and bought it without a thought. So much for established writers, but what about a newcomer like you?

You need to show that your book has credibility. Of course, the fact that it is the fruit of sober research is a good start. But what else can you add? Are you in good contact with specialists in the field?

---

[2] Personal correspondence. Email to the author, 2 June 2023.

[3] Personal correspondence. Email to the author, 3 September 2023.

And not just ivory tower experts, but, most importantly, with practitioners too – people who are 'hands-on.'

Have you spoken at conferences or given workshops or talks? Are you an advisor to a related ministry? Before you worked on your thesis, what did you do? Do you have experience in the past that helps give credibility to your work? If your book concerns the plight of the untouchables in India, then the fact that you worked amongst them for three years is relevant and gives credibility to your writing.

Do you have a social media following? If you do, any potential publisher will be excited to know about it. Immediately, you have a channel to promote the book, but also the added credibility that comes from your interaction with people who are following you.

Do you know people who would be willing to write a book recommendation or a 'blurb' for the cover of the book? Avoid getting a bland 'blind recommendation' from someone who hasn't read and interacted with the book. Instead, find someone willing to read the manuscript and interact with you, the author.

In the Christian context, and depending on where and how you will be published, you will probably need to share your 'Christian credentials.' Do you belong to a denomination? Do you occupy a position within a church structure? Have you taught at a recognised seminary? Have you worked with a Christian ministry? Your family also counts: can you share something about them? Is your spouse a well-known figure? Or one of your parents? Or one of your children?! For many people, without famous connections, it could simply help to share that you have one husband, two cats, three dogs and sixteen children…

In recent times, publishers have often included extra background notes about the writer that have nothing to do with the content but can help readers relate to them as people: that the author runs ultramarathons, is a jazz enthusiast or is keen on French cooking. A publisher may like to include an appealing photograph of the author. These matters depend so much on the social culture in which the book will be released, on the style and focus of the publisher and perhaps whether the author (you) is photogenic or not!

PUBLISHING FOR ACADEMIA

As academic book editor William Germano says, 'Revising your dissertation for publication is about expanding that population of readers so that it becomes broad enough for a publisher to take your manuscript and turn it into a book.'[4]

In some specific cases, a thesis has been accepted almost in its entirety to be published as a book because the focus of the research has been directly applicable to a wide public, and it has been written in a style appropriate to that same group of readers. In other words, the population of readers does not need to be expanded. Much will depend on the nature of the area of research and the approach taken in the dissertation itself.

In the history of academic publishing, doctoral dissertations have also been published in their entirety as complete books because of their unique contribution to a field of study. A Cambridge University thesis by Imre Lakatos on the philosophy of mathematics was published as a slim volume called *Proofs and Refutations*.[5] Though dealing with what seems like an impenetrable area of study, this ground-breaking work was written as a narrative; a series of dialogues between a group of students. It has since been translated into many languages and is considered essential reading to date.

Your thesis may not reach the stratospheric heights of an Imre Lakatos, but it might warrant publication as a whole if it makes a significant contribution of interest to a specific readership. In general, though, 'the dissertation is a not-yet-book,' as William Germano notes.[6]

PUBLISHING AN ACADEMIC ADAPTATION OF THE THESIS

Most academic publishers produce 'de-dissertated' versions of research. While a complete thesis might fit in a university library,

---

[4] William Germano, *From Dissertation to Book*, second edition (Chicago, USA: University of Chicago Press, 2013), p13.

[5] The 1976 book *Proofs and Refutations: The Logic of Mathematical Discovery* (Cambridge: Cambridge University Press, 1976) is based on the first three chapters of Lakotos's 1961 four-chapter doctoral thesis, *Essays in the Logic of Mathematical Discovery*.

[6] William Germano, *From Dissertation to Book*, second edition (Chicago: University of Chicago Press, 2013), p20.

few academics would have time to read pages of detail and will need a much clearer presentation of the results.

Addressing scholars from elite secular universities in the US who want to publish fruit from their dissertations, experienced academic editor William Germano writes: 'When a dissertation crosses my desk, I usually want to grab it by its metaphorical lapels and give it a good shake. "You know something!" I would say if it could hear me. "Now tell it to us in a language we can understand!" It isn't the dissertation I want to shake, of course, it's the dissertation's author. The "us" I want the author to speak to isn't just anyone, either, but the targeted readership that will benefit from a scholarly book.'[7]

He goes on to say: 'It's hard to pick up a dissertation and hear its author's voice. Dissertations don't pipe up. Like the kid in the choir who's afraid she cannot carry a tune and doesn't want to be found out, the dissertation makes as small a sound as possible. Often that sound is heard by a committee of three to five scholars, and no one else. Revising a dissertation is partly a matter of making the writer's text speak up.'

In some academic fields, such as philosophy and history, scholars with clear Christian commitments have been published by major 'secular' university publishing houses such as Oxford, Cambridge, Harvard and Yale. Being published by them might be something to aspire to!

Evangelical theological education in the US and Canada has increased since the 1960s. As Christian universities and centres of advanced study have developed, so has a demand for serious academic work with a Christian focus. As Andrew Le Peau notes, evangelical academic publishers, such as Eerdmans and IVP Academic, have grown to meet this demand.[8] One factor for their growth has been that they have offered lower retail prices than university presses and, particularly, specialised publishers in Europe.

---

[7] Germano, *From Dissertation to Book*, p18.

[8] Andrew T. Le Peau "Evangelical Academic Book Publishing: 1970-2020," in Derrick, Stephanie (editor), *Chasing Paper: Critical Reflections of Christian Books and Publishing* (Eugene, OR, USA: Cascade Books, 2021), p96.

In some regions of the world, Christian academic publishing (and research in general) is in its early stages, and publishing a highly academic work would be difficult. As a result, many graduates from the developing world want to publish their 'converted' dissertations in the North, using English. In these cases, the scholar must control the copyright of their work to be able to publish content from the thesis in their home continent, either in English or in a local language.

Writing for a broader audience does not mean that the content needs to be trivialised or oversimplified. In the Christian world, there is a huge appetite for books that communicate content and meaning without being overly technical. Throughout Christian history, both scholarly and more general books have been important.

Martin Luther wrote theological arguments in Latin – directed at the scholars of the established church – and at the same time, he wrote for the broadest possible public, using a lively German language, and often with illustrations by Albrecht Dürer. Scholars debate which had the greatest impact on the growth of the Reformed Movement: the academic publications or the popular pamphlets and books!

In the Case Studies section, you can read testimonies of scholars who have seen the fruit of their labours published for both academia and the wide church.

4. MOTIVATION

An author needs to have in mind the potential readers of the book. A reader needs to feel that the book is addressing a 'felt need' and that the writer is qualified to help. The way the author presents his or her credentials will depend on the nature of the books and also the motivation of the author that pushes the project along.

MISPLACED MOTIVATIONS

One obvious misplaced motivation is that getting a book published will provide a source of income. Royalty income from books is normally modest, if not minimal. Some authors do become rich through their writing, but few will reach the sales of JK Rowling. A few years ago, a UK secular writers' organisation reported that the majority of its members lived below the poverty level! Publishing a book can generate a useful income, which could be used to help pay for a new laptop, for example, but it would not be wise to focus primarily on the money.

In some situations, the very fact of having a book published can have financial implications, even though few books are sold. For some seminary or college teachers, there is automatically a salary increase for each book published. This may be the norm in only a few countries, but in many universities, a regular rhythm of publishing is necessary to maintain tenure.

Vanity can be appealing. There is something extremely satisfying about seeing your name in print on the cover of a book. Some people find that even more gratifying than being addressed as a 'doctor.' Becoming known as the author of a book can be a good way to impress your friends and neighbours. Left lying on your coffee table or office desk, your tome might generate admiring compliments. And of course, the question of what presents to give to your loved ones for Christmas and birthdays could be solved!

VALID MOTIVATIONS

Putting aside thoughts of financial gain or a sense of importance, a key consideration should be the *impact* of a published book in the church, in helping the Body of Christ stick close to Scripture, to be refreshed and renewed in the power of the Spirit and energised for action and mission in service.

- In this case, you could reinforce the message of your book with further reading suggestions.

The published book might serve to ***challenge*** Christians to think biblically and to develop a 'Christian mind' and so 'not be conformed to this world, but be transformed by the renewal of your mind' (Romans 12.2). Too often, Christians adopt the thoughts and responses of the society around us, rather than developing a renewed mindset. In *To Change the World,* James Davison Hunter writes that the Christian church has frequently reacted to the 'world' in a simplistic way and has failed to engage culture effectively.

- Include links to organisations that would help readers respond actively.[1]

For many involved in Christian service, the publication of a book can be a way to ***develop a ministry*** and extend its reach and influence. The book can help an author become established as an expert in an area of work. This is a valid motivation, to be taken up with modesty. It is perfectly correct that you should seek – in all humility – to make known your experience and sound theology and so 'to equip the saints for the work of ministry, for building up the body of Christ' (Ephesians 4.12).

- It would make sense to include information about and links to your ministry.

Sometimes the simple fact of publishing a book can ***open doors*** to interesting opportunities. Authors living in small towns might find themselves interviewed for the local newspaper, radio or TV. In some areas, book launches, with local dignitaries or even the President in attendance, are organised and can be wonderful

[1] James Davison Hunter, *To Change the World: The Irony, Tragedy, and Possibility of Christianity in the Late Modern World* (Oxford: Oxford University Press, 2010).

opportunities to be a witness and to share the good news of the gospel.

- Make sure you include contact details!

The potential ***influence*** of a published book is a great motivation. The evangelical church needs a greater Christian presence in academia. So, if you are moving into work in an academic field, it would be important to make the most of your thesis. It would help if you aimed to get it published in the most appropriate possible place, where it will have the most impact. Don't 'waste' it!

- Connections with those working in the field, especially endorsements from them, could help.

It may be that your dissertation contains elements that can engage with society in general, that will ***connect*** with people who are not Christians, helping them to understand a Christian viewpoint. In these cases, it might be wise to think at the outset about contacting a 'secular' publisher.

Author Philip Yancey, commenting on the state of Christian publishing, and the occasional million-copy-selling title, asks: 'Is Christian literature penetrating culture, or is the fissure separating Christian readers from the broader public yawning ever wider?'[2] The writer CS Lewis wrote books that connect with and penetrate culture. His Narnia series, as well as the science-fiction novels, attracted a wide audience, as did his essays on the world situation and the question of suffering. His books built bridges connecting the society of his day with the Christian message. Maybe your thesis-turned-book could do something similar in our time.

- Check your language so that you don't include evangelical slang!

---

[2] Philip Yancey "Christian Publishing: Too Many Books & Too Few Classics?: Christian Writers Often Express Their Theological Concepts without Emotion, Drama, or Tension", *Christianity Today*, March 2, 1984. p20.

Any of these factors could affect the way that the content of the book is developed, the type of language is used and the way that the final work is presented.

OUR CHIEF MOTIVATION

Our motivation then, in producing a book goes beyond any thoughts of financial gain or passing fame. The book could help strengthen a ministry and have an influence on society. It could provide solace to readers and help answer their deepest questions. It should respond to the genuine felt needs of your 'public.' Underlying both our motivation and the process of writing will be the desire, as Christians, to do everything 'as unto the Lord.' Philip Yancey writes:

> *Christian writing is not simply a self-expression to further our careers and egos, but rather an expression of Truth and an offering to the Father of lights. It's time we writers realized that the quality of our work becomes an integral part of its message. And, it's time for Christian readers to show concern when that message gets smudged.*[3]

In the Old Testament, key artisans in the construction of the place where God would be worshipped, Bezalel and Oholiab, were filled with the Spirit of God to work with skill and creativity. Their work was to draw attention to God, not the artist (Exodus 32 and 35). Writing with guidance to new churches, the apostle Paul calls slaves to work for their masters not with a grudging spirit, nor cutting corners, but 'as serving the Lord' (Colossians 3.23-24). This revolutionary concept was fundamental to the witness of the Early Church amidst a pagan society.

Fame is alluring, but the story of the widow's mite (Luke 21.1-4) reminds us that it doesn't matter if no one sees what we do. Ultimately, it doesn't matter if we don't get recognition. A writer can cling too tightly to their ownership of a written work, with an over-concern to guard or to copyright a written text. Scripture calls us to give generously, to the point of giving ourselves away. We should

---

[3] Philip Yancey, *Open Windows,* Thomas Nelson Inc, Nashville, Tennessee, 1985. Chapter 7 'The pitfalls of Christian writing', p90.

be able to delight in seeing others take up ideas that we have researched, even though no credit is given to us.

The composer Johann Sebastian Bach wrote an extraordinary number of works, week in and week out. In his own time, these received little recognition, yet today they are known as masterpieces. His guiding vision was to produce music that honoured God. He wrote *soli Deo gloria* (only for God's glory) on each sheet of music. Can we do the same – metaphorically speaking – on each page of our book manuscripts?

5. Making the Text Work

Now that you have a clear idea of the core message of your book and of the public you are aiming to reach, it will be time to work on the text itself, to turn it into a better shape to serve as a book. It might be helpful to think of two levels of revision: structural and internal.

Structural engineering, surgery or 'broad brush' editing
To start with the general structure of the book proposal, and with the key message you want to communicate, there will be a lot of sections that can simply be eliminated. Miriam Adency of Regent College, Vancouver writes:

> *'How to Turn Your Dissertation into a Book'. This was the title of a workshop offered by the University of Chicago Press at an annual conference of the American Anthropological Association. Sixty eager PhDs crowded into the room, clutching their dissertations. The editorial advice was drastic: 'Throw out the first three chapters of your dissertation.' What dreadful words. Yet, as the editor explained, 'the first chapters of a dissertation contain the statement of the research problem, the methodology, and the historical review of research in this field. Your general reader is not interested in all this. He won't stick with it. He'll quit reading. So you have to skip to chapter four or so, where you introduce your fresh discoveries. Start there. That's what will hold your reader.' A thesis does not make a good book, but a thesis may contain the ingredients for a wonderful, life-changing book. The material must be reworked following guidelines for effective writing. And in the end, even those ponderous early chapters may yield gleanings which can be served up to the discerning reader in footnotes and appendices.*[1]

Holding clearly before you the core message that you want to communicate, choose those sections of your thesis that will work to

---

[1] Miriam Adeney, Regent College, Vancouver, 'Training Leaders to Write' (unpublished manuscript), c1990.

back up that key idea. These then can form the basis of your chapter headings.

Sometimes it is not clear in which order the chapters should flow. It is best not to worry too much at the outset, since you can always shift them around later, adapting any linking passages or ideas. Some writers find it helpful to use brainstorming or mind-mapping techniques to help them work out a logical sequence of chapters and their connections.

Some dissertations lend themselves to a clear structure. For example, with history writing, the very chronology provides a 'through-line' to the text. Equally, some doctrinal studies start with the Old Testament, then the New, the Early Church, and so on.

While the original bibliography, which was important to show your sources, has probably already been scotched, it might be useful to explain where more information can be found and to give reading suggestions. If you feel that some readers would appreciate a full academic bibliography, you can always put this on a website and include the link somewhere in the text of the book.

Technical terms should either be eliminated or explained well. After all, your aim is not to impress your readers with your superior command of arcane knowledge or ancient languages. If some technical terms are needed, it can be helpful to create a glossary for easy reference. If needed, a modest number of Hebrew or Greek words could be included, with transliteration and explanation. It may be best not to include footnotes. Their content can be incorporated into the text itself. If it is essential to include a footnote, place it at the end of each chapter or the book itself.

DETAIL EDITING, WORKING WITH THE TEXT

Good writing includes rewriting and simplifying, eliminating repetition of unnecessary words and cutting unnecessary digressions. As well as being readable, a shorter book will be cheaper to produce and more likely to be published.

Clear the Ground

Once you have a clear structure for your publication and have dealt with the issue of over-technical language, reduce 'fog' or eliminate 'fillers' and tighten your sentences.

- Eliminate words such as 'very' and 'really'; also unnecessary use of 'the' and 'that'
- Remove (most) adverbs and adjectives
- Replace long or complicated words with short ones
- Split long sentences in two. Often conjunctions ('and,' 'or,' 'but' and 'however') are used to connect two independent statements that can often be rewritten as two sentences.

If you can remove words without losing the sense of the statement, delete them. There is a worked example of the great effect of eliminating fillers in the Appendix by David Cranston, on minibooks.

Write (Re-write) with a Specific Reader in Mind

Having a clear idea of *who* your book will be aimed at, you can write or re-write in a style appropriate to that public. Focus on your niche and write in a way that conveys your voice. It can help to hold an image of a potential reader in your mind. If your book is going to be aimed at rural pastors in your country, think of a pastor you know and imagine talking to him or her. If you have a picture available, you could always stick it above your desk as a reminder!

Give Life to Your Text

Academic writing can tend to be bland and lacking in 'life.' Here are eight suggestions that could help give vitality to your writing.

1. Think of each chapter as a mini-drama[2]

Open the chapter with a story that illustrates the problem, then explore the issue and give examples that show how the problem is resolved. Think in terms of *story arc*, moving the reader from

[2] Albert Hsu, 'Writing for a General Audience,' unpublished notes shared with potential authors by InterVarsity Press, Downers Grove, Illinois. Shared with permission to cite, in personal correspondence with Ellen Hsu, 24 February 2023. p1.

problem to solution, from question to answer. Without being too mechanical or forced, you can always conclude a chapter with the solution to the problem in the opening story.

2. Develop each chapter like a sermon point[3]

Another idea is to invoke the example of a Spurgeon or a John Stott! Include a healthy mix of exposition, illustration and application. As Hsu says, these don't need to be forced into a slavish pattern, but make sure you both *show* and *tell.*

3. Put yourself on the page

Laura Portwood-Stacer recommends that writers converting a dissertation into a book should write so 'that it feels like you are showing up on the page.' Editors like strong distinctive voices that will be 'good company' for the duration of the book, which is a lovely way to think about the writing style we should aim for!

4. Provide a variety of illustrations

These can be biblical or contemporary, personal or third-person, individual or corporate. Illustrations help root ideas in the real world in a way that relates to readers' lives. Readers need to see themselves in the text. Give readers multiple examples to connect with, both from your experience and of others too.

5. Adding visual features

Many readers find visual material to be very helpful. These could include summary tables, simple sketch maps, schematic diagrams, figures or sidebars. Apart from their intrinsic value, they will also help to break up blocks of text that might appear to be dense. It would be unusual to see a cartoon in a dissertation, but why not in your book?

6. Check your 'signposts'

Beware of unnecessary 'signposting.' You don't need to tell your readers that you're going to tell them a story, or that this story will illustrate a certain point: just tell the story. On the other hand,

---

[3] Al Hsu, 'Writing for a General Audience', p1.

'guideposts' can be extremely helpful to your reader at the start of any new section that includes more difficult material, with a summary of the theme of the section, why it is important and how it will be tackled. Likewise, a well-worded summary could help the reader understand the road they have just travelled on.

7. Revise your verbs and nouns

Use vigorous and active verbs; avoid the passive. Avoid overusing the same word – find a thesaurus and keep it close! Use concrete nouns and specific details if you can.

8. Make it flow

It is important to make sure that the sections and the chapters are not just connected by logic. Instead, they should flow forward from one to the next. As Germano says: stage your ideas 'so that they develop a rhythm instead of moving jerkily like a poorly projected silent film.' Writers of thrillers know how to write with a beat, with a steady pulse of energy that keeps the reader interested. Changing the metaphor, a dissertation being turned into a book is like a complex piece of music; your job is to make the major themes sing out.

One simple tip is to read each chapter out loud! You should be able to hear the cadence of your voice. Adjust the text until it reads well and sounds like you. Then, if you are feeling brave, and if you do happen to have an extremely patient friend or spouse, you could always read it aloud to them too, asking for their comments as you go along. Someone has even suggested you preach from each chapter!

NEXT STEPS

Make a plan

Many writers find it a challenge to return to the manuscript to improve the writing. As Germano says: 'Highly intelligent people are adept at a lot of things, including making excuses for avoiding things they know they need to do.' And: 'It's too easy to think of it like the big jigsaw puzzle on the dining room table – every time you pass through you fiddle with a few pieces, and once in a while you finish a bit of sky or the edge of the house. But you rarely worry about deadlines with a jigsaw puzzle.'[4]

You may well not have an external deadline to keep, but to avoid a cycle of procrastination, which can lead to irrational feelings of guilt or frustration, it helps to make a plan. Include time for investigation, sharing with interested groups, discussion with publishers and revision. Make a plan that is realistic and which will help you keep moving.

Field test your material

Our son works in software development, in which it is normal to 'stress test' programs or websites under diverse situations to find weaknesses or mistakes. They will also want to see how users react and how well they will understand the software. Writers too can 'stress test' their work as they talk over key ideas with good friends, listen to their responses and use those inputs to refine the elements of the planned book or article.

Share your material in a real-life settings, like a Sunday school class or small study group. By doing this you will discover connections between your content and the real-world situations of your audience. You might be able to write a short article to sound out interest in your subject and to help you 'make the text work.'

Peruvian writer and theologian Samuel Escobar wrote: 'We don't need to worry about writing for academics and the intelligentsia. The challenge is to write so that the people who matter may understand.' Well-loved as an excellent communicator, Samuel was asked by one interviewer about some of the formative influences on his ministry:

> *His key training ground, he said, was the two-year period he spent as a junior school teacher. When you work with children you know if you are communicating or not, they will soon tell you! Anyone who has heard Samuel speak will know that he also communicates with great warmth, which in person is expressed by a broad smile. A clear message, expressed with warmth*

[4] Germano, *From Dissertation to Book*, p77.

> *and clarity: characteristics that are important when working with children… But true of all good writing.*[5]

CS Lewis and JRR Tolkien were members of a writing group nicknamed The Inklings, which met one evening a week in Oxford. Members shared ideas about their projects and read sections aloud. Famously, they often disagreed. However, the open sharing helped to sharpen their work and to stimulate new ideas.

You may not have access to a group like The Inklings, but you can take opportunities to share your work with others. Why not set up a 'focus group'? Invite a few friendly pastors around for a coffee and cake, for you to share a section from your potential book. Seek out honest friends. It can be painful, but listen to caring advice from others, then simplify your work and self-edit as you go along.

PRACTICAL DETAILS

The introduction

It will be worth giving special attention to the introduction, which is often written when the rest of the book has been completed. It should be a warm and welcoming place, to invite the reader in. It should establish an intriguing problem or issue. One important recommendation: don't give away the conclusion!

The foreword

A foreword for the book, written by someone well-known, can be a very powerful help in making the book stand out. This could be your dissertation overseer, particularly if your supervisor is well-known within their discipline as an expert. Other times, they might suggest for you a foreword from someone else in the field who is well known.

Titles and subtitles

Chapters and sections should be balanced and of a manageable size. Subtitles should be useful signposts to guide the reader through the

---

[5] Samuel Escobar, *Mi peregrinaje con la palabra* (text document circulated by IFES Latin America, 1998 – my translation).

text. An interesting piece of advice from Germano is: 'Walk through the chapters and notice where you get tired.' These should also be listed on a contents page, normally placed at the front of the book.

Conclusion

Quoting Germano again: 'Most attractive conclusions mirror without repeating what has gone before, recall to the reader's mind the voyage you have made and come to a rhetorically satisfying end.'

Acknowledgements, dedications and other matters

A page of acknowledgements or dedications can be placed at the start or end of your book. It is a way of thanking those who helped you get to this point. In the end section, you would place an index (if needed) and a bibliography or a list of suggested readings.

Appendix

Sometimes important material that isn't key to the structure of the book might make a better appendix than interrupting the flow of the book.

Endorsements

Think creatively to identify the right person to help the book gain more visibility. It would be wise to find someone who has name recognition not necessarily in your academic field, but within your target potential readership.

6. Publishing Options

The options available for publishing your work have multiplied in recent years, and they continue to change from year to year. You might want to publish your book through a ***traditional publisher*** or opt for ***self-publishing***. Then there are other routes to consider with so-called ***hybrid publishers***. The situation can be confusing, and it is worth spending time considering the options, searching on the web and seeking wise advice. First, here are some general issues to think about!

ARTIFICIAL INTELLIGENCE (AI)

Artificial intelligence (AI) is already built into many of the tools that we all use when writing, such as spell-checking options in word processors and applications such as Grammarly. These resources are helpful and unproblematic.

Regarding deeper content development uses of AI, there are complex issues concerning copyright and transparency. Generally, the AI engines are not claiming copyright, but they may produce something which is closely based on copyright material and therefore could expose publishers to copyright infringement litigation.

Several publishers, therefore, are asking writers to affirm that they have not used AI in the course of producing their work, so the best course of action is to be reticent in your use of the technology. If you plan to work with an established publisher, the best thing to do would be to talk with the publishing house about what might be appropriate boundaries for the use of AI.

DIGITAL PUBLISHING

Years ago, it was said that the printed book would die, as readers would opt for digital formats such as Kindle. That has not happened. During the years of the Covid pandemic, sales of printed books increased as readers found pleasure in not using a screen, but in handling and even smelling(!), a well-produced printed book.

Some categories of books are indeed no longer printed. Decades ago, encyclopaedia salesmen would visit door-to-door, offering fabulous multivolume sets of encyclopaedias or dictionaries, along with bookshelves to hold them! In the age of Wikipedia, no one now buys such enormous and expensive editions. Another great change has been in academic publishing, in which a majority of books are now published digitally.

In many parts of the Majority World, books are not read by only one person, but are passed on from hand to hand. Hence, one copy of the book can end up blessing many. So the printed book has its advantages over electronic books, which cannot easily be shared.

As we shall see, many books today are published in both printed and digital formats. Many popular books available on sites like Amazon are available in print, digital media and also on audio. But that is another story!

Copyright

One issue that concerns many writers is copyright. It is a complex issue which varies from country to country and changes as governments change or as technology impacts information dissemination. In some countries, you automatically hold copyright and in others, you have to assert this.

Essentially, copyright is the right to copy. In book publishing, it is a protection for the creator of the text. Once an idea is in tangible form, the copyright owner holds the sole right to copy the material or to allow others to copy it – even in translated form. Copyright is the legal right granted to you when you create an original work. It's a form of 'intellectual property' which you can sell, license to a publisher or a producer, or leave in your will to your loved ones.

Copyright protection does not last forever. Most Western governments maintain the protection for 50 to 70 years beyond the author's death. After that, copyright protection usually ceases, leaving the text in the 'public domain,' so anyone can then use and publish it. Often, however, a copyright on the typesetting and page layout requires negotiation with the original publisher.

Perhaps the key point to be aware of is handing over your copyright to a publisher rather than *ceding* the publishing rights.

PUBLISHING RIGHTS

The copyright belongs to the original creator of the book, while the publishing rights are given, usually sold, to others by the copyright owner, allowing them to reproduce the work. Every publisher has to purchase the rights to create books in a certain format (paperback, e-book and so on.) They also have to purchase or at least gain permission for the rights if they want to publish a book in a different language.

So, be aware of handing over your copyright to a publisher rather than the publishing rights.

Specific concerns have been reported by scholars from the Global South who have been drawn into an agreement to publish in the North and who have unwittingly relinquished rights. As a result, their work is published only in a very expensive edition, and they are prohibited from producing a de-dissertated edition which would be of service to the wider Christian community.

OPEN-ACCESS BOOKS

To make research as accessible and discoverable as possible, and to achieve greater impact, several major academic publishers are offering the publication of books under an open-access licence, which enables readers to download the work and at the same time protects the author's copyright. This means that you own the right to the work, and you decide the type of licence that will be applied to your open-access book.

A Creative Commons licence (or CC licence) is a public copyright licence that enables the free distribution of otherwise copyrighted work. In other words, it describes how others can share, reuse and build upon your work. There are six types of CC licences and all of them require the user to attribute the original work back to you. You might recognise some of the licences if you check the usage rights field in the advanced settings of a Google image search.

All CC licences include these first two acronyms: CC: Creative Commons (the type of licence); BY: attribution (the copyright holder must be acknowledged). You might also see 4.0 being mentioned – this is the current version of the licence, and it is updated by Creative Commons every few years.

One advantage of using a CC licence is that it is clear to readers what you are allowing them to do with your work – without them needing to contact you directly for permission. Creative Commons is a not-for-profit organisation whose goal is to increase the amount of openly licensed creativity. Creative Commons chapters exist in many, but not all, countries of the world.[1] As a good friend says: this is the kind of creative hybrid model that navigates global inequalities in knowledge production and consumption.

PUBLISHING A COMPLETE THESIS

There are highly reputable and well-established academic publishers in Europe, such as Brill (Netherlands), Peeters (Belgium) and Peter Lang (Switzerland), which publish selected and peer-reviewed theses, aimed at academic and university library sales. If you have the opportunity for your dissertation to be produced in that way, your academic colleagues will be most impressed.

But do bear in mind that the resulting book will typically be very expensive, and well out of the reach of the general public. While publishing in this way might not cost you anything financially, bear in mind that in most cases authors receive little in payment through royalties from these sales.

Potentially more serious is that, in some cases, authors assign the rights to the academic publishing house to publish the complete thesis and in doing so make it impossible (due to contract law) for the author to produce a simplified version of the work for a broader audience.

In some countries, there are university presses which at times publish complete theses, in particular from staff related to that same institution. In recent years, with the options made available by on-demand publishing technology, there are also newer publishers which specialise in producing selected theses for publication.

It is important in all these cases for the author to study the contract and conditions offered by any such publishing house and seek wise advice from colleagues in the same academic field to

[1] Information on the global publishing industry is updated regularly on the Publishers Global website: https://www.publishersglobal.com/#.

understand the limitations that could be placed. It would be wise for you to maintain the right to publish your research in different formats and other languages, without impediment.

PUBLISHING A SECTION OF THE THESIS

There is not necessarily any simple relationship between the size of a dissertation and the end-of-process published resource. Some massive academic tomes can provide material for a couple of interesting articles for a general reader, while some shorter guided research projects might grow into a helpful full-length book.

It is possible that one *section* of a dissertation could be of interest to an academic publisher, while other parts would be of interest to a wider public. If the more 'academic' part is relatively short, it might be more appropriate to present it to an academic journal. Part of a thesis could work alongside other chapters in a joint publication. In either of these cases, the partial publication could lead to future opportunities to publish either at an academic level or for a general audience.

Several colleagues have warned that great care should be taken when approached by a seemingly scholarly journal. Authors should ensure that such publications are internationally recognised and peer reviewed. As always, great care should be taken to ensure that publishing rights are maintained. Colleagues in the same field and the home institution should be consulted, along with a thorough online search.

7. WORKING WITH A PUBLISHER

According to Publishers Global, there are over 20,000 publishers and publishing services companies based in 132 countries. Leading the field by country are the United States, Germany and the United Kingdom. Leading cities that are centres of publishing are London, Paris and Barcelona. To some, book publishing is a major global business, worth billions. To others, it is pure passion, fired by a love of text, graphics, typography and even paper. Publishing today is complex, challenging and fascinating. There are so many different types of publisher, each with its own philosophy and business model.

TYPES OF PUBLISHER

The global, big-business publishing world is dominated by a small number of international communication giants: at the time of writing, **the 'Big Five'.** Each owns a raft of publishing companies, each with its niche. Several well-known Christian publishers are now owned by one of these global giants. They are happy for each daughter company to maintain its own ethos and specific market, as long as it brings in a profit. A Christian book with a mass-market appeal would fit well with this group.

There is a sector of **university, academic and organisational publishers**, with a non-profit remit, which aims to produce books that contribute to society and culture. This group includes high-prestige publishers, such as major university presses. Many academics aspire to appear on their lists. An academic publisher would be open to publishing a book by a Christian writer if it is of sufficiently high calibre and interest to academia.

Amongst the **major Christian publishers**, some have a denominational or doctrinal stance; others are interdenominational. Some are well-established with many employees; others are smaller presses, possibly with a niche readership. Within this group, differences include the strength of their marketing and distribution networks and also their capacity to work with authors to develop titles.

Then there are **many Christian publishers** in every part of the world, sometimes with a very focused publishing plan. Many are motivated to serve their area with books that are relevant, contextualised and biblical. Many do find themselves with limited resources and the need to take great care in the books they publish. As a potential author, you will need to approach them with thought and care, considering this reality, but also with an awareness that you could be working alongside a publishing team that genuinely cares for God's people and God's glory.

HOW EDITORS DECIDE WHAT TO PUBLISH

Every publishing company has its particular ethos, focus, theological emphasis and capacity to distribute. An author must investigate potential publishing partners with care, studying the details of particular emphases on their website and talking with knowledgeable contacts.

In general terms, here are some factors that publishers of all types will take into account:

- Format, genre and topic. They will ask: does this fit in our list? Do the overall purposes and perspectives of the manuscript fit with our publishing house? For example, is the book (and the publisher) charismatic or non-charismatic, reformed or dispensational, denominational or nondenominational, popular or academic?
- Quality of writing. Will a lot of copy-editing be needed? Are there misspelt words or poor grammar? And is the writing dull?
- Quality of content. How good is the overall quality of the ideas in the proposed manuscript? Will the book have a significant ministry? Are the ideas ordinary or fresh? Does the author have credentials? Is there a maturity of understanding?
- Potential market or audience and financial feasibility. Are we able to reach enough people to break even or make a profit?
- Finally, some subjective factors: the appearance of (and absence of mistakes in) the cover letter! Knowing the author. The editor's schedule. The author's teachability.

ADVANTAGES OF WORKING WITH A TRADITIONAL PUBLISHER

Some of the positives of working with a traditional publisher include:

- Prestige. Traditional publishing offers a sense of validation. Even if your book doesn't sell very well, if it is published by an established publisher, you will have that stamp of approval, which will serve you well with future projects, or at least with your self-esteem.
- No cost. Traditional publishers do not charge authors. If they accept your book, they will want it to succeed to repay their costs through sales and to pay you royalties.
- Credibility with booksellers. Bookstore managers will typically support a traditionally published author but hesitate with a self-published one.
- Industry knowledge. Traditional publishers will be knowledgeable about what makes a book attractive and interesting to a reader. They will have learned from their successes and failures.
- Marketing and distribution. An established publisher will already know how to promote and market books using all sorts of channels, from gaining book slots in serious newspapers to producing TikTok videos. They will also know how to distribute them, dealing with shipping, customs, accounts and returns.
- Greater possibility of being produced in translation and other media. Some books may be attractive to publishers in other language regions. A traditional publisher will have the contacts and the 'know-how' to make these connections, which could help generate extra income for the author, as well as serve as a blessing for more people.
- Another potential outlet for the book could be as an audiobook, a sector of publishing which has grown rapidly in recent years as 'delivery' online has become the norm. A traditional publisher should already have links with an audiobook publisher.

Some negatives of working with a traditional publisher are:

- A possible or felt loss of control. When authors sign a contract with a traditional publisher, they are typically 'ceding' rights to their work.
- Delays. The path to becoming traditionally published can be meticulous and painfully slow. If you need your book to be out for a conference at the end of the year, this option may not be for you.

CONTACTING A PUBLISHER

If you decide that the best option for you is with a book publisher, then start by taking time for investigation. Find out more about a potential publisher: look at their website and consider the type of books they produce, including their theological stance. Talk to your peers and ask for advice. Ask your friends or colleagues who have been published if they could give you the e-mail address of their editor. Go to academic or ministry conferences, stop by the book sales area and make contact with a publisher.

Publishers are looking not only for authors who have established reputations but also for those on the rise. A publisher may take on your publication not only because of the dissertation itself but also because of you and your potential as a future writer.

Your first contact with the publisher should be with a concise and well-written letter, giving some essential details of the book project. It may seem an obvious thing to say, but when you do make this direct contact with a publisher, make sure the letter is well written! A badly written letter will at most elicit a wry laugh from your would-be editor who receives it, as it is crumpled up to go in the bin!

The letter should set out clearly who you are and what you have done, followed by a very brief outline of your proposed book. Do not send a manuscript until they ask for one. Rather, send a one-page summary of your book, highlighting the key message; explaining how it differs from other books in the same area; explaining your credentials; and letting them know if you have a presence on social media or access to interested groups. Make sure you write the summary well, in good English (or whatever language you use) and use an attractive, clear layout.

If your dissertation has already been published in another language or region, or if you hope to do so, it would be good to mention it at this stage. It is important to be transparent, especially if you can indicate that these ventures help to make the book a stronger prospect for publication.

Be patient and wait to be asked for more. If you do receive a rejection letter, don't be put off. Try to learn from the experience and any feedback they may give you.

In some circles, you might hear of writers working through a 'literary agent,' someone who represents you to publishing companies. It is reported that most of the big 'secular' publishing houses that produce fiction will only take agented submissions. The agent is part lawyer, promoter, coach and sounding board. Legitimate agents only get paid when you get paid, and they receive 15%, which is the industry standard. However, in the Christian publishing world, especially regarding the type of book that results from a dissertation, the employment of an agent is not common.

If you are from the Majority World, then do search out local publishers, who often work against great odds to keep serving and surviving. They may do a far better job of promoting and selling your book in your area. They may not be able to pay huge royalties, but you could have the enormous delight of seeing your book change lives and impact communities in regions you know. Bear in mind too that writers who are successfully published in their home country are much more likely to be accepted for editions in countries such as the UK or the US.

WHAT COMES NEXT?

Publishing contracts are complicated, and everything is negotiable. Talk to the publisher about what's important to you. Do you care about foreign rights? Audio rights? The contract you are first sent should be seen as a starting point for negotiations. Don't sign it. Don't automatically accept everything the publisher suggests. Make sure you understand the small print of the contract and are happy with it before you sign.

Once accepted, your publisher will want your book to be at its very best, in content, readability and presentation. So the manuscript will pass to the editorial team, where it will pass through the stages of editing, which can include:

- Developmental editing. This is big-picture editing: looking at the structure and the logic of the book.
- Line editing. Sentence-level or stylistic editing: looking at the form and flow of the text. Also cutting out any unnecessary words, reducing 'fog' and making your writing sing.
- Copy-editing. Sentence-level editing: checking layout, spelling, punctuation, grammar.
- Proofreading – once the book has been typeset. This is micro-editing: spotting errors, bad line breaks and other oddities. Some publishers will ask you literally to initial every page to 'sign off' on the proofreading.

Most publishers will want to decide on the book title, but hopefully, their choice will fit in with your style. Sometimes, enigmatic or intentionally intriguing wording is chosen. In any case, both the title and any subtitle should be welcoming so that someone seeing the cover on a bookstand will think 'I need to check out that book.'

Likewise, the publisher will decide on the cover design. You might have good ideas that can be shared with the design team, but the publisher will have the last word. After all, they are the ones who are investing a lot of money in your book! If you do have interesting graphic material that could be introduced into the cover, such as photographs (for which you hold the copyright), then this would be the time to share these.

Some publishers expect non-fiction books to carry indexes, and in some cases it is expected that an author will pay for an index, as it is an extra. In this case, it is helpful to think about the purpose and audience of your book and who would find an index useful. Will the index get enough use to justify the cost in either money or time? Index entries are made up of three main elements: main headings, subheadings and locators (usually page numbers). When authors create their indexes, it can be hard for them to view the work from the outside and to tell what would be most useful. Thus, common pitfalls include indexing either too much, too little or with unhelpful entries. This is a matter to talk over with your publisher. Freelance indexers are available if needed.

Hopefully, you will have already identified the ideal person to write a foreword to the book. The publisher will also want you to find people who can write brief recommendations or endorsements, which could be placed on the back cover or the first interior pages. These details will be important to decide on as the cover design is being developed.

Many decades ago, it was common for authors to leave the project with the publisher, who took on the tasks of book promotion and distribution while the author could retire into anonymity. That has all changed. In the present environment, the identity and profile of the author are fundamental to the book's distribution and sales. The marketing team will need you to collaborate in the promotion of the book through your presence on social media and in such activities that are appropriate to your field.

8. SELF-PUBLISHING

Working with an established publishing company has never been the only option available to writers. In 1759 Laurence Sterne self-published the first two volumes of *Tristram Shandy*. In 1843 Charles Dickens, unhappy with the royalties he earned from Chapman & Hall for *Martin Chuzzlewit*, self-published *A Christmas Carol*, selling an initial print run of 6,000 copies in weeks. In 1941 Virginia Woolf chose to self-publish *Between the Acts* using her own publishing company, Hogarth Press.

Many writers, and not only those who are turning a dissertation into a book, will empathise with the sentiment in the recent Writers' Guild guide to self-publishing:

> *You're thinking of writing a book, or have written it and want to get it published. The only problem is that traditional publishers are either not taking submissions or are not interested in your work...You may well have considered self-publishing but have been put off by how complicated it all seems. You might not feel confident about technology or think it will cost too much to do. Indeed, when you are published by a traditional publishing house, a lot of the work is done for you and you automatically work with editors and illustrators, publicists and so on. Thus, it can feel daunting to consider doing the job for yourself.*[1]

Times have changed and since the 1990s technical developments have impacted the world of publishing. One is the availability of accessible publishing software, enabling a computer user to 'typeset' a book without a deep knowledge of traditional typesetting. Also, printing technology has developed, allowing direct file-to-print services. In more recent times, the rise of self-publishing platforms has empowered even more authors to publish their work without relying on a traditional publishing company, or even a print shop.

---

[1] Writers' Guild of Great Britain, *Self-Publishing: A Step-by-Step Guide for Authors* (London: Writers' Guild of Great Britain, 2023), p4.

There are different approaches you can take when it comes to self-publishing:

1. Do-it-yourself self-publishing. You have full control and do most of the work, occasionally drawing on others to undertake specific tasks. There are self-publishing service providers which can help with individual tasks such as editing, designing, producing and marketing the book.

2. Assisted self-publishing This is a more expensive option, and you may have less control, but you could find it easier if you're not comfortable about going it alone. You engage a company to manage the whole project.

Under either approach, you should maintain the rights to your book. If a sales platform is used, the writer should receive all profits after the distributor has taken its agreed percentage and the writer should be able to extract themselves from the agreement at any time.

1. Do-it-yourself self-publishing

If you have a niche community or audience in your locality, who are interested in reading your book and with whom you have direct contact, then a private print run could be a good option.

The simplest place to start would be at a print shop where you live. Printing companies vary in their expertise and not all can produce books, so ask around. If you are printing locally, it would be wise to visit and look at samples. Beware the printer who will tell you that the unit cost per book will go down with a longer print run. On the whole, people don't buy books because they are cheap, but because they believe your book will benefit them in some way. So be careful not to print more than you can reasonably sell in a year.

An increasing number of printing companies have incorporated print-on-demand technology, making it possible to produce short runs of books. Alternatively, you may decide to use a print service at a distance, using a print-on-demand service, or to produce an e-book on Amazon, without any intermediary.

Whichever route you decide on, you will need to supply the computer files for the book interior and the book cover, so you will need to decide who will edit and also design the book. The steps involved are:

1. Get the book edited

Assuming you have already self-edited the book, return to your manuscript and take time to revise it again. It might be wise to find someone who can do this editing for you.

2. Think of a great title

You need your book title to be snappy, evocative and fitting for its genre. It should grab people's attention, and the book should do what it promises. Think, would you pick it up if you saw it on the shelf? Short titles tend to be best. Then maybe an explanatory subtitle a little longer. It's also good to check other titles that are around, to make sure you aren't duplicating or too closely referencing another work. Look on Amazon! Ask your family and friends for ideas!

3. Format the interior

The next task is to format the interior of the book according to the means of publication chosen. For example, if you opt for a print version, you must check paper size and margin widths with the printer. While professionals design book interiors using software such as InDesign, the formatting can be done using standard word-processing software such as Word or economical alternatives to InDesign such as Affinity Publisher. These programmes can be challenging to learn, so it might be worth finding a freelancer to help out.

Resist the temptation to use unusual fonts. The legibility of your text is essential. Avoid using upper case letters, which seem TO SHOUT AT YOU and are harder to read. The ascenders and descenders of lowercase text help readers distinguish words. Choose a typeface that is elegant and clear. Similarly shaped letters and characters can also increase letter confusion and decrease readability for people with dyslexia or visual impairment.

4. Get the cover designed

In this highly visual age, a striking cover design and graphics are essential. Some authors have enjoyed producing their covers, while others have opted to work with a designer. You will need to decide on any text you want included in the design and also think about the message of the book and how that should be represented through the cover design. Most of all, the title of the book (hopefully short) and the name of the author (you) should stand out on the cover, and other design elements should help potential readers understand what the book is about.

5. Have the whole book proofread

Now that you have both the interior typeset and the cover (front, back and spine) of the book ready, this is the time for proofreading. Often skipped by the over-optimistic, this micro-editing and checking are important for spotting errors that have crept in, resolving bad or embarrassing line breaks and sorting out other oddities. Don't forget to check the details on the cover: even professional book designers have made embarrassing mistakes on book jackets.

6. Get the book made

Traditional paper-and-ink printing by 'offset'

You can opt for normal or 'offset' printing, but you will need to factor in storage space and costs and also think about what happens if you are unable to sell all your books. You will also need to pay a fee upfront to get all your books printed. However, in return, the unit price for each book will be undoubtedly less than you would obtain through print on demand (see below).

Producing an e-book

This need not be difficult and there are upsides to self-publishing this way:

- There are lower upfront costs, as you will not need to pay printing costs and you do not need to factor in storage or transportation costs.

- Many of the e-book platforms are free to use, and you can use more than one of them. Each operates slightly differently, but they all provide detailed guides on how to use their service and on how the files should be formatted. There is a standard e-book format called EPUB used by most distributors except Amazon, which uses MOBI format. You can hire freelancers to format your e-book or do it yourself before you upload it to your chosen distribution site.

Print on demand (POD)

Print on demand, sometimes abbreviated as POD, is a fulfilment system in which books are printed only after they are ordered by the customer. The benefits of this are:

- Only enough copies are printed as needed, so you don't need to worry about storage space and costs
- It reduces your upfront costs
- It's a more environmentally sustainable way of using resources.

However, POD can lead to higher prices for your readers or lower profit margins for you, because the unit cost of printing each book is higher than printing in bulk. It also means your books are unlikely to be stocked in bookshops, as they usually prefer to have the option of returning unsold books to the publisher.

7. Registering your book

The details of book registration vary from one country to another, but an ISBN (International Standard Book Number) is universal.[2] This is a code used to identify your book and its specific edition. In many countries, you are not required by law to have an ISBN for your book, but they are used by publishers, sellers and libraries to order, stock and list your book, so they are extremely useful. Some book printers can process an ISBN; otherwise, the ISBN agency of your country should be contacted. Incidentally, if you opt for offset printing, you will need the ISBN before the book is printed, as the

[2] https://www.isbn-international.org.

number is used to generate the barcode that printed books carry on the back cover. In many countries, your work is automatically protected under copyright law once an ISBN is granted. It is therefore good practice to use the copyright symbol (©) on your work, alongside the year it was created, to actively display your intent to claim copyright protection.

8. 'Marketing and promotion'

How will the reader find out the book exists and be able to get hold of it? Strive to make contacts with all possible interested parties to sound out who could review and promote the book.

When you self-publish, you will need to seek out your testimonials or endorsements by sending copies to reviewers. You can do this before printing, by sending a PDF of the formatted text. This way you might be able to include recommendations on an interior page or the book cover.

Consider sending details to any journals you know, local newspapers, church newsletters and your own mailing list.

9. Selling your book

Some people find it embarrassing to promote and sell their own book, but with the right attitude, this can be fun. Here are some well-tried options:

- Offer to give workshops or conferences on the subject of your book, with the book available for sale.
- If you teach courses, use your book.
- If you work at a Bible college or seminary, make sure there is a book display somewhere, in your own office or at the reception.
- Make contact with relevant ministries and organisations.
- Ask family and friends to help as salespersons!
- At your own home, have a book display by the door, so that visitors can purchase a (signed) copy before they leave.
- Maybe a local shopkeeper could have some on offer, next to the cash desk.
- Even better, at a local bookshop.

- At your church, present a book table, with the offer to sign copies.
- Ask church pastors you know to give a two-minute book spot from the pulpit.
- In some countries, there is a local independent writers' guild where authors can share advice and sometimes club together to present books in a book fair.

E-books are hosted on a publishing platform. Amazon's Kindle is the largest of these and Kindle Direct Publishing, or KDP, is Amazon's e-book publishing unit. At the time of writing, IngramSpark is a popular publishing platform that could be used by DIY self-publishers. It distributes books to most online bookstores. Bricks-and-mortar stores can also order books from IngramSpark at wholesale prices for sale in their venues.

It may sound contradictory, but it can help to give your books away to selected readers, as long as they will then recommend your book and generate sales. For a similar reason, do not worry about piracy or digital rights (DRM) used to prevent digital copies. Trust that, as the public learns about your book, by whatever means, they will want to purchase the real article.

2. ASSISTED SELF-PUBLISHING

If you feel that the demands of totally DIY self-publishing are not for you, you don't have to do all of the heavy lifting. The services available from self-publishing 'service providers' could be the answer. These are companies that arrange for the interior and cover design, prepare your book, for printing using print on demand (POD) and also as an e-book, as well as distribution and marketing. Naturally, these services carry a cost.

Two of the benefits of working with an assisted self-publishing company are:

1. It saves time. Publishing a book requires a huge investment of time. If you don't have any time to spare, it makes sense to hire a company that can do it for you.

2. It saves sanity. Book publishing is also complicated. If you aren't interested in learning new skills, pay someone else to do it for you.

When looking for a one-stop-shop self-publishing company, don't sign up with the first one you see. Be careful of unscrupulous companies looking to scam you out of your money. Look for a self-publishing company that has a clear upfront fee and is transparent with the prices for their services. Steer clear of companies that ask you to e-mail them for a quote. Choose a company that claims *no* rights to your work. You are self-publishing, which means that you should retain all rights to your work.

At the time of writing, the following companies have been reported as reliable. All of these companies will help you with print and e-book formatting, design and distribution.

- Blurb
- BookBaby
- Draft2
- Gatekeeper Press
- Lulu
- StreetLib[3]

One-stop-shop self-publishing companies can help you turn your manuscript into a printed and bound book, but they won't determine whether your book sells. Only you can do that. You won't generate lots of sales unless you work creatively and strategically.

Despite the company's marketing promises, it's unlikely that your book will make it into a brick-and-mortar bookstore. Self-published books rarely make it to bookstores. But that's not a big deal, because self-published authors can use the internet as a direct-to-consumer distribution channel.

---

[3] For more information on these companies and to compare their services, go to their websites: https://www.blurb.com; https://www.bookbaby.com; https://draft2digital.com; https://gatekeeperpress.com; https://www.lulu.com; https://www.streetlib.com.

It will help to have a good e-mail database to send out attractive promotional materials. Established social media platforms such as Facebook, X, Instagram and TikTok[4] are all being used by publishers and reading groups. Undoubtedly, new platforms will appear, and it will be worth keeping an eye open for those suitable for promoting books.

Be persistent. It is natural to make a splash when the book is first released, but sometimes it takes time for news of a publication to reach a wider audience. Once it has been out for some time, you may wonder how you can continue to promote a book. A publicist friend talks of 'creating book news.' If you are invited to give a presentation of the book, if your book is reviewed in a journal, or even if your book is referenced by someone else, any such event is an opportunity to share a brief note via your mailing list, website or on your social media, to keep the book on the reader's horizon.

Keep monitoring information about your book, too. For example, if the book is sold on Amazon, you should check and refresh the information as often as possible. The pages on Amazon for many Christian books are meagre in information, with limited information about the content, few reviews or recommendations and no detail about the author. There is nothing unethical about encouraging your friends to post a review or recommendation on the site!

Be aware of unscrupulous or predatory 'hybrid,' 'contributory,' 'paid-for' or 'vanity' publishers.[5] It can sometimes be difficult to tell the difference between these publishers and companies that offer genuine self-publishing services. Unethical, paid-for, vanity or contributory publishers will purport to undertake some or all of the publication services, but the key difference is that they will insist that you assign to them some rights in the book. The fees that they charge are also usually much higher than those being offered by a genuine self-publishing company. The Writers' Guild of Great

---

[4] Media Makers Meet, *TikTok for Publishers: Thoughts, Stats and an Exploration*, https://mediamakersmeet.com/tiktok-for-publishers-thoughts-stats-and-an-exploration/.

[5] See: Mary DeMuth, 'Fifteen Traits of Predatory Vanity Publishers,' Mary DeMuth Literary (2022). https://marydemuthliterary.com/vanitypublisher/.

Britain (WGGB) and the Society of Authors have released a report, *Is it a Steal?*, warning against these practices.[6] As they note, with unscrupulous, vanity or contributory publishers, it is very unlikely that you'll ever see a return on your investment, and they should be avoided at all costs.

SUMMARY: PROS AND CONS OF SELF-PUBLISHING

Some positives of self-publishing are:

- Faster publication.
- Potentially higher earning.
- Control.
- Unfiltered promotion.

Some negatives of self-publishing are:

- Cost. DIY self-published authors pay out of their pocket to create a book.
- Less editorial support.
- Less marketing support.
- Less distribution support.
- Lack of recognition.
- Required storage room!! If you opt for DIY paper-and-ink printing.

As we have seen, the option to self-publish your book can be extremely effective, depending on your circumstances and resources of time and finances. A crucial aspect will be your ability to communicate details of your book with your potential readership. Self-published authors may receive a cold shoulder from the media and some readers will be reluctant to look at a book that doesn't come from a reputable publisher.

A final thought. In 1843, when Charles Dickens self-published *A Christmas Carol*, he felt free from the publishers' 'penny-pinching,'

---

[6] Writers' Guild of Great Britain and the Society of Authors, *Is it a Steal? An Investigation Into 'Hybrid'/Paid-For Publishing Se'vices* (London: Writers' Guild of Great Britain and the Society of Authors, 2022).

but then designed so gorgeous a book – with fancy bindings, gilded pages and lavish illustrations – that, despite it being an instant hit, the author barely broke even. So, be careful to budget well!

9. Hybrid Publishing

There are now also alternative models of publishing that sit between traditional publishing and self-publishing and which are generally known as 'hybrid.' With **hybrid publishing**, the publisher and author collaborate to share costs and risks. The author may be required to surrender some control and rights in return for the publisher's financial and other contributions.

Within the category of hybrid publishing, there are many varieties. Some are fairly close to traditional publishers but expect the author to do more of the work, relinquish royalties or provide some funds. Given their financial limitations, many respected publishers in the Global South expect authors to partially or fully fund publication. These funds could come from the writer's resources or through an interested agency. There are groups who, after a book is acquired, help their authors crowdfund their books to cover costs or produce books using an open-source platform.

There are many shades of grey and potential traps for scholars seeking the best way to publish their dissertation transformed into a book. So, first a note about vanity publishers and other predatory groups to avoid.

Vanity publishing

A common criticism of hybrid publishers is that they are vanity presses in disguise. In vanity publishing, which has been in existence for a long time, the author pays for the cost of all services and also signs a restrictive contract which usually involves surrendering significant rights. These groups will exploit an author's dream to see their book in print, sending excessive praise about the work and writing about their excitement at the opportunity to work with you. They might also describe their approach as better than traditional publishing or self-publishing – or even present their approach as the way the industry works now.

PREDATORY PUBLISHERS

One group of vanity publishers can be correctly described as predatory publishers. As well as sending flattering messages and making vague promises they cannot fulfil, they charge excessively large sums for services and take your publishing rights so that you cannot publish the work elsewhere. Sadly, some vanity publishers purport to be Christian ministries and claim to be serving the Kingdom. Any scholar who aims to publish their work to benefit the church, develop a ministry or acquire credibility should be aware that working with a predatory vanity publisher will accomplish none of those aims. These so-called publishers should be avoided at all costs.[1]

ETHICAL HYBRID PUBLISHING

Having set out a warning about vanity and predatory publishers, let us return to genuine and ethical hybrid publishing!

Given the increased fragility faced by publishers in every part of the world, many have adapted their business model to transfer some financial risk into the hands of the author. Under a hybrid publishing model, the publisher and author share the costs of publishing and distributing a book. The publisher is responsible for producing and distributing the book, while the author pays a fee to cover some or all of the cost of the component services.

It has been suggested that the best test for whether a company offers assisted self-publishing services or hybrid publishing is to ask if, in the process of self-publishing, money and rights are controlled by the writer. If a company offers services to the author without claiming any rights and allows the author to control the entire process, they are assisting the author to self-publish. Whereas, if the company takes some rights, they are a hybrid publisher. They will do this because their long-term investment in the project is greater.

A legitimate, ethical hybrid publisher undertakes editorial evaluation, setting standards in what work it accepts for publication based on quality and merit, in the same way that a traditional publisher does. By contrast, a vanity press will publish any book for any author, regardless of the quality of the work or its potential,

---

[1] See: Mary DeMuth, *Fifteen Traits of Predatory Vanity Publishers.*

provided the author meets the cost of publication. An author whose work is accepted by a true hybrid publisher can therefore have more confidence that the project is worth implementing.

ACADEMIC HYBRID PUBLISHING

In recent years, several academic publishers, including those that produce biblical or theological titles, offer hybrid publishing options. For many scholars, the prospect of being published by an acclaimed serious publisher is very attractive and would look good on a curriculum vitae. Such publishers may have access to the academic library market, and so assure the author that their work would be distributed in academia.

But do bear in mind that a book published under a hybrid model by a major academic publisher could turn out to have a high selling price, well out of the reach of the general public.

The Christian publishing company Wipf and Stock offers authors diverse models of standard and hybrid publishing, with Cascade operating like a traditional publisher, Pickwick focusing on specialised publications and W&F offering hybrid options.[2] A very different model is Lexham Press.[3] Their website notes: 'By entering the Christian market from a digital-native position, we have a history of creating innovative resources designed for and integrated into the Logos platform.' Lexham now incorporates Weaver Book Company.

As these two examples show, there are many options available now, and the situation is constantly evolving, with changes in technology and public interest. Authors are recommended to take time to search using the web and also to speak to as many wise advisors as possible.

Few of us enjoy reading contracts, but before jumping into an agreement with any publisher, it is important to read and understand the details. By all means, look for help from a friendly

---

[2] Information about publishing with Wipf and Stock Publishers, including a downloadable Proposal Form, can be found on their web site: https://wipfandstock.com/submitting-a-proposal/.

[3] The Lexham Press website includes an online Manuscript Submission page, https://lexhampress.com/manuscript-submission.

lawyer or an experienced writer. Move forward with your eyes open and be very clear about your motivation, your message and the 'market' of the public that you have a concern for. Beware of making a snap decision based on flattering e-mails and promotional material. Think deeply and pray hard.

Whatever option you choose, remember that, whatever a publisher might promise, books don't sell themselves. You should consider carefully how you will communicate details of the publication and news of your book.

10. Building a Platform

'One of the most significant changes in the publishing process is the shift of marketing from publisher to author' writes Sandra Van de Vicht,[1] senior editor and publisher at Zondervan.

Book publishers today expect their writers to have a 'platform' – 'a place to stand on which you can be seen' – and from where potential readers will hear about your research and your book, and then hopefully buy the book. If you plan to self-publish your book, then some sort of platform is all the more necessary, as you will not have the benefit of the promotional machinery of a publishing house.

This may sound like 'marketing' talk, and in the strict sense, it is. You will probably need to sell your book, but that doesn't mean adopting a hard-sell approach. The famous business consultant and management guru Peter Drucker insisted that, 'marketing aims to make selling superfluous. Marketing aims to know and understand the customer so well that the product or service fits him [or her] and sells itself.'[2]

Platforms exist on social media, websites, blogs or podcasts. All are means to develop contact with readers and stimulate interest in the content of the book. The platform might include additional or supplementary material and reviews of the book, as well as activities of interest by the author, such as upcoming conferences, courses or media appearances. It could also include links to relevant organisations and connections to the platforms of colleagues, as well as links to previous publications and courses or institutions that have adopted your work.

---

[1] Sandra Vander Zicht, 'Thirty Years of Change in Christian Book Publishing', in Derrick, Stephanie (editor), *Chasing Paper: Critical Reflections of Christian Books and Publishing* (Eugene, OR, USA: Cascade Books, 2021). p108.

[2] See, for example, Peter Drucker, *Managing the Non-Profit Organization: Principles and Practices*, Harper Perennial, 1990.

All this can sound very demanding. Is it all necessary? Mary DeMuth writes of how in the publishing world the idea of building an author brand was popularised in the early 2000s. After branding discussions, the word 'platform' began to circulate around the year 2007. As she writes: 'Whereas my books used to wholly be evaluated on the concept, the potential audience, and how well I wrote and articulated the book, now it mattered how "famous" I was.'

She concludes her piece by writing: 'So I'm personally shifting from the word platform to the word **presence**. What can I do to help others? How can I reach those who really want to hear, see or read my content? And most importantly: how can I bless those in my fold? And how can I do so without losing my mental health or my precious, limited time?'

So, building a platform or opening channels of presence can happen organically, through your immediate contacts and opportunities. Proactive ways of developing a platform, and becoming better known, could include writing book reviews and articles for journals or magazines, presenting papers at academic conferences and speaking to lay or less-specialised audiences. Active membership in professional or ministerial groups can also be helpful. In some contexts, writers have found opportunities to write for local newspapers and appear regularly on local radio programmes.

In her case, Mary DeMuth maintains a modest platform without being obsessed with the latest social media crazes. In all this, as DeMuth says, the most important is prayer. Here are some ideas that could help you to develop a modest platform:

GROW A MAILING LIST

One of the most effective means of communication with your friends and with a public interested in books is still by using e-mail, so build an e-mail list and send updates. It is not wise to add names to a mailing list without permission being asked, but it is not complicated to create a 'sign-up form' on a mailing programme such as Mailchimp, or you can add details manually to those contacts who have permitted you to do so.

PRODUCE AN INFORMATIVE FLYER

Your publisher, if you have one, may produce a one-page flyer, otherwise you can create one easily, using free software like Canva. Then, share this flyer with your colleagues and friends, at a conference, via e-mail or anywhere else you like, with details of your book and how they can get hold of it.

CREATE A WEB PAGE FOR YOUR BOOK

Again, if you are working with a publisher, a web page may already exist; otherwise, it is not difficult to create a web or blog page, using a free resource such as WordPress. There, you can include information about the book, explain where the book can be purchased, offer free resources or articles and show a personal profile.

The web page address can then be linked to anyone who will be happy to include it, in your e-mail 'signature' and on social media. One good piece of advice is to look at other writers' sites and see what you think works. Have a way for readers to get in touch, but not with your home address! Be creative. Writer Ruth Downie comments: 'Have some attractive cards or bookmarks or something to give out for free that have your website address on them.'[3] (To promote a book on Roman Britain, she once gave out free woad seeds with the website address printed on the packet.)

USE SOCIAL MEDIA

You can post details about your book and a link to your web page on Facebook, Twitter (X), LinkedIn, Academia and any other social media account. Use social media to connect with others who work in the same field and also as a source of ideas for continuing research, by asking questions to others in your niche group. On Facebook, you could create a page specifically for the book. Know the hashtags your potential readers use and employ them well.

If you feel comfortable in this world, become what George Veletsianos calls a 'networked scholar.'[4] Some serious publishers now are promoting books on TikTok, but maybe that would be a

---

[3] Personal correspondence, 25 November 2023.

[4] George Veletsianos, *Social Media in Academia: Networked Scholars* (Abingdon, UK: Routledge, 2016).

step too far for you! Many serious publishers are now using TikTok to reach a wider audience and even form reading groups, so if you have friends who are good at this sort of thing, it could be fun to follow their lead and produce a video!

SEND OUT REVIEW COPIES

One friend writes: 'I'd still send out review copies as if you get a decent review it gives you something to quote in publicity. Even if the review isn't entirely good, you can legitimately quote the bits that are.'

CHECK DETAILS

If your book is being published by a traditional or a hybrid publisher, make sure that the metadata they are using for your book is accurate and attractive. If you are self-publishing, it would be good to find out what metadata is and how to use it! If your book is on Amazon, make sure you set up the free author page through Amazon Author Central. Here you can include more information about your book, your ministry and anything else that is relevant. Similarly, on Goodreads, if your book is mentioned, you can add information through the Goodreads Author Dashboard. An author friend recommends you do that but then adds: 'Never read Goodreads reviews if you want to stay sane.'

ACADEMIA.COM AND RESEARCHGATE

These are profit-making services which disseminate research material. They will invite you to pay to research using their databases, but this is probably not worth it. On the other hand, at no cost, you can upload articles or even information flyers to your publications. It can be fun to be notified of users worldwide who have read them.

It can feel uncomfortable to highlight your credentials. However, it is not a question of 'blowing your own trumpet' but rather sharing such information that helps potential readers understand that you have something valuable to say and that you can be trusted. If you feel it could help, you could ask a close and objective friend to help you prepare a succinct and modest summary. But not too modest!

The tension between presenting credentials and displaying modesty is not new. In several of his letters, the apostle Paul set out his credentials, but always for a good reason: to correct false teaching. At the same time, he presented himself as a sinner saved by grace, aware of his weakness, and as a fellow slave with his companions in Christian service.

Reviewing all the options open to us today Mary DeMuth concludes: 'My best advice… is this: pray. Ask God to show you the avenues of presence that will best help others in your audience. Let go of anything that is no longer serving you, or is bringing you harm… Think about your audience as your congregation and seek ways to serve them simply and powerfully. Ask yourself, "What would help my friend today?" And then, do it.'

11. Making a Decision

In prayer, consider how best the publication will serve the church or the wider community, and how it will help develop a future ministry. Guiding principles come from God's Word: **We are called to serve.** Following the example of the Lord (Phil. 2:7) and the apostle Paul (Phil. 1:1, 1 Cor. 3:9), we remember that we are servants. So, when, where and how can we best serve? How best can the book be used to serve? **We are stewards of thc gifts given to us.** We have all been given gifts (1 Cor. 12:15-18), and these are to serve others (1 Peter 4:10). How best can I use the gifts God has given me? In what way will this book help develop the gifts God has given me and given to others?

And we are also **part of the Body of Christ.** John Donne wrote 'No man is an island,' but sometimes, as Christians, we act as if we are. Rather, we are part of the Body of Christ and rightly dependent on others. Do we have wise Christian friends with whom we can share our plans and dreams?

As a consequence of being part of the Body of Christ, many of us have connections around the world. The healthy growth of the church is fundamental to its response to both spiritual and physical needs. Assuming your book will contribute to changing lives and strengthening the church, there might be friends in the Global Church who can stand with you in some way as your book project is developed.

In your home country as well as other areas you know, there may well be church groups, interdenominational ministries, aid organisations and mission agencies that in some way can support your project without creating dependency. This help could be:

- By providing an endorsement for the book, to be quoted on the cover;
- Allowing the organisation's name and logo to appear on the back cover, to communicate the book has friends!

- Making a pre-publication commitment to buy a certain quantity of the books;
- Agreeing for the book to be promoted through their social media or news bulletins;
- Planning a book launch meeting for you to present the book;
- Contributing something, however small, to the costs;
- Joining you in prayer for the project.

Nobody can make these connections for you. Pray, investigate, knock at doors. In the present world, in which few have the opportunity for full-time theological study, and even fewer have the privilege of a period of advanced study through a Bible college or university, Christian literature offers an extraordinary opportunity to contribute to the formation of new generations of Christ-following disciples.

Don't fritter away opportunities. You have enjoyed the tremendous privilege of a time of deep study. You have struggled to write your dissertation. Now may you be given the grace, the humility and the wisdom to be able to enrich the Body of Christ using the printed word by producing one or more accessible books out of the riches of an academic thesis.

Appendix: Case Studies

The case studies that follow reflect a range of experiences encountered by scholars seeking to publish their work for a wider audience. They may give you ideas for further exploration. Unless indicated otherwise, the comments are from each writer.

Federico G. Villanueva

Home country: Philippines

Title of thesis: 'The Uncertainty of a Hearing: A Study of the Sudden Change of Mood in the Psalms of Lament'

Degree: PhD, awarded 2007

Degree awarding body: University of Bristol, United Kingdom

Thesis published as *The 'Uncertainty of a Hearing': A Study of the Sudden Change of Mood in the Psalms of Lament*

Publisher: Brill, 2008

The book for a wider audience based on the thesis – *It's OK To Be Not OK: The Message of the Lament Psalms* – was published first in 2012 by OMF Literature and then later by Langham Publishing (2016). This book has also been translated into Spanish, Chinese and Bahasa Indonesia.

Federico writes: 'Langham Publishing now publishes PhD theses in the monograph series. Of course, these go through a review process and not all get published. There was no Langham Publishing when I sent my work to Brill. It was my supervisor in Oxford who suggested and recommended my thesis. For a scholarly work, Brill is good, though not for accessibility. I receive very little from the sales of my book in Brill, but it gave me some introduction to the scholarly community, which we also need.'

On developing the thesis for pastoral audiences: 'One of the things that helped me publish this book based on my dissertation was the fact that it was my own pastoral experience that led me to research lament. Thus, it was not a huge gap to turn the central message of the dissertation into a more popular book for the church. The central question of my dissertation came out from one of my

Bible study groups in a slum area, when one of the members whose house had just been burned down asked a powerful question. That question formed my central thesis. We must listen to ordinary people. The deep ideas and the good ones are often not found in the libraries, but out there, where the people are, especially the poor.'

CHRISTOPHER M. HAYS

Title of thesis: 'Luke's Wealth Ethics: A Study in Their Coherence and Character'
Degree: DPhil, awarded 2010
Degree awarding body: University of Oxford
Academic monograph published based on the thesis: *Luke's Wealth Ethics: A Study in Their Coherence and Character*
Publisher: Mohr Siebeck, 2010
Popular book published based on the thesis: *Renouncing Everything: Money and Discipleship in Luke*
Publisher: Paulist, 2013
In Spanish: *Renunciar a todo: el dinero y el discipulado en Lucas*
Publisher: Puma, 2019

Christopher writes: 'Having published a full academic version of the thesis freed me up (psychologically!) to write a little popular book. The approach to writing *Renouncing Everything* that (I think) served me well was to write it mostly out of my head. I made a short outline (maybe a couple of pages) of the entire book, and what I wanted to accomplish in each chapter. Then, without outlining, researching, or citing anything other than Scripture, I drafted each chapter entirely out of my head. For academic work, I would never do that. But since you have lived with the thesis for years, you probably don't need to create a detailed outline, you already know how the argument fits together. This approach – drafting a chapter entirely based on what was in my mind – was liberating and made for a much more accessible work. Of course, I edited it afterwards and added in some light footnoting. But trusting what I already knew allowed the argument to flow well.

'Finally, my experience as a New Testament scholar was that I needed to bracket out some of the practical/personal/moral/spiritual applications of scholarship when writing the thesis. That's appropriate for an academic work. However, the popular work gave me space to include an additional chapter of spiritual/ethical reflections. It was a joy for me to add that, and I think it made the book better (both because it wasn't just a restatement of my monograph and because it responded to the personal questions that my academic research invariably raised for believing readers).'

MONIQUE M. INGALLS

Title of thesis: 'Awesome in This Place: Sound, Space, and Identity in Contemporary North American Evangelical Worship'

Degree: PhD, awarded 2008

Degree awarding body: University of Pennsylvania

Book published based on the thesis: *Singing the Congregation: How Contemporary Worship Music Forms Evangelical Community*

Publisher: Oxford University Press, 2018

Monique writes: 'I found William Germano's *From Dissertation to Book* very helpful in the early stages. For finishing the project, it was also immensely helpful to receive a residential research fellowship. I spent a semester with no teaching responsibilities, and with supporting faculty and student colleagues giving feedback on chapter drafts.'

SAMUEL TEDDER

Home country: Finland

Title of thesis: 'Children of Laughter and the Re-Creation of Humanity: The Theological Vision and Logic of Paul's Letter to the Galatians from the Vantage Point of 4:21-5:1'

Degree: PhD, awarded 2018

Degree awarding body: Durham University

Book published based on the thesis: *Children of Laughter and the Re-Creation of Humanity: The Theological Vision and Logic of Paul's Letter to the Galatians*

Publisher: Cascade, 2020

Samuel writes: 'With the finished work, and about half a year after being awarded my PhD, I approached one publisher first, the Library of New Testament Studies, in August 2018. The feedback was good, but the recommendation was to publish the thesis as several articles or approach another publisher, since they took only very few manuscripts to publish in a year. This first round took about five months. I was not ready to break my thesis into a series of articles, so I approached another publisher, Wipf & Stock, in February 2019.

'They saw my work as having the potential to be appreciated by a wider public and having a solid grounding in rigorous research. Hence, they accepted it to be published in their Cascade imprint. This gave me the benefit of getting an assigned editor to work with me, and they also did the finishing touch with the copy editing. My editor gave me a very helpful framework for how to revise the thesis into a book: first I needed to trim some branches (sections, paragraphs), and then work on cutting and shaping the leaves (sentences). I also needed to translate all the foreign-language sentences into English and transliterate needed references from Hebrew and Greek. This all took a lot of work and time, but it was also motivating and rewarding to see my work get a more concise and sharp form. In the process, I also added some new material that reflected my further thinking on the issue, especially in the conclusions. The whole process from approaching the publisher to it being finished took about one year and two months. The result was very satisfying, and I am very pleased to have worked with Wipf & Stock to get my thesis out as a book.

'After my book was published, I got some feedback from a reader who appreciated my book but felt that it was still for a more specialised audience. In hindsight, if I wanted my PhD research to benefit an even wider audience, it would have needed more time or reflection to better bridge the distance from an academic mindset to a pastoral mindset that seeks to grasp what this is saying to us now. I have done that in my teaching and preaching but did not quite reach it with the book. I am more and more convinced that serious study and research of the Bible should be for the benefit of the church and its mission. Hence, I hope that with a possible other book, I can write better to reach and relate with the audience that would use it best.'

DARÍO LÓPEZ RODRÍGUEZ

Home country: Peru

Title of thesis: 'Evangelical Church and Human Rights in Peru: A Critical Evaluation of the Theology of Mission of the National Evangelical Council of Peru from 1980 to 1992, with Special Reference to Its Understanding and Practice of Human Rights'

Degree: PhD, awarded 1997

Degree awarding body: Oxford Centre for Mission Studies/Open University

Darío's research on human rights in Peru was rooted biblically in a study of social justice in Luke's gospel. Building on his research, Darío has published eight books on subjects including human rights from a biblical perspective, and studies on Luke's gospel. Darío writes in Spanish, but one title has been published in English translation: *The Liberating Mission of Jesus: The Message of the Gospel of Luke (Pentecostals, Peacemaking, and Social Justice)* (Pickwick Publications, 2012).

INI DORCAS DAH

Home country: Burkina Faso

Title of thesis: 'Birifor Women Communicating the Gospel: An Analysis of Birifor Women's Contribution to the Growth of the Church in West Africa (Burkina Faso, Côte d'Ivoire and Ghana)'

Degree: PhD, awarded 2015

Degree awarding body: Akrofi-Christaller Institute of Theology, Mission and Culture

Book published based on the thesis: *Women Do More Work Than Men: Birifor Women As Change Agents in the Mission and Expansion of the Church in West Africa (Burkina Faso, Côte d'Ivoire and Ghana)*

Publisher: Regnum, Africa, 2017 and Wipf and Stock, USA, 2018

Ini Dorcas comments that it was a good experience to learn how to turn a thesis into a book. A mutual friend notes: 'She has achieved the notable accolade of publication both in West Africa and the Global North. Furthermore, she is a female African Christian scholar publishing on the role of women in African Christianity.

ADAM SZUMOREK

Home country: Poland

Title of thesis: 'Seeing and Showing the Unseen: Towards a Methodology of Utilizing Cognitive Linguistics in Biblical Preaching that Employs Metaphors and Images'

Degree: PhD, awarded 2019

Degree awarding body: University of Chester

Book published based on the thesis: *Seeing and Showing the Unseen: Using Cognitive Linguistics in Preaching Images and Metaphors*

Publisher: Langham, 2023 (published as a Langham monograph)

Adam writes: 'When deciding about the degree of changes in the process of converting a thesis into a book, it is essential to keep in mind the audience and potential readers. In the case of my book, I was thinking about more academic readership; however, I believe that there is a lot of content that could enrich a less academic preacher's methodology of sermon preparation or even approaching the text. Thus, I use some examples and ideas from other books and think about a much shorter publication about communication and imagination that would use some of my PhD material.

'It is also important to work closely with the reviewers and editors, who can suggest or introduce some changes. In my case, many of my reviewer's comments were helpful, but considering differences in our approaches and our preferred linguistics theories, applying all of the reviewer's comments would result in writing a completely different book with a completely different theoretical framework.

'On the other hand, working with Langham editors was a pleasure. We discussed every step and each change. I expected them to introduce more changes in my text since it is my first publication in English. They did not change much.'

BETHANY MCKINNEY FOX

Title of thesis: 'Disability, Healing, and Jesus: Perspectives and Practices from the Gospels'

Degree: PhD, awarded 2014

Degree awarding body: Fuller Theological Seminary

Book published based on the thesis: *Disability and the Way of Jesus: Holistic Healing in the Gospels and the Church*
Publisher: IVP Academic, 2019

Bethany notes that her writing style, even for academic purposes, tends to be accessible. She prioritises generosity as a writer toward her readers, so she tries to make things clear and readable – even in a dissertation format. She writes: 'So I didn't have to do a whole overhaul or anything. I maybe added some more examples, and then adding a clear introduction to give people a sense of the book and orient readers was also really important. Beyond that, I'd just say not to get discouraged if you initially get rejections from publishers, and that it's worth waiting to find one that's excited about your project and not one you have to talk into it.'

Appendix: Resources

Recommended Reading

For those interested in a broad picture of Christian publishing, this collection of essays by senior publishers from around the world is fascinating reading:

Stephanie Derrick (editor), *Chasing Paper: Critical Reflections of Christian Books and Publishing*, Cascade Books (2021)

For more on the technicalities of converting a thesis into a book, in both cases written for those aiming for academic work in US universities, these are highly recommended:

William Germano, *From Dissertation to Book*, 2nd Edition, University of Chicago Press (2013)

Laura Portwood-Stacer, *The Book Proposal Book: A Guide for Scholarly Authors*, Princeton University Press (2021)

On writing in general and improving your style, there are many books available. Here are some classics that are often recommended:

William Zinsser, *On Writing Well: The Classic Guide to Writing Nonfiction*, Harper Perennial, anniversary edition (2016)

William Strunk and EB White, *The Elements of Style*, 4th Edition, Pearson (1999)

Sol Stein, *Solutions for Writers: Practical Craft Techniques for Fiction and Non-Fiction*, Souvenir Press (2023)

Software

Some famous writers still use a mechanical typewriter or even pen and paper, but for most of us, who don't have a secretary or amanuensis, a basic computer will be the simplest option. Standard word-processing software such as Word (MS) or Pages (on a Mac) are powerful programs which some people find almost too full of options. A simpler text-based program with a clean-sheet look and fewer distractions might help the writing process. Here are some programs that have been suggested by writer friends:

Scrivener is a favourite writing tool for many authors of both fiction and non-fiction. It uses a helpful outline structure, enabling the user to move quickly from one section to another, with a clear overview. With space to add notes and reference files, Scrivener helps you to focus on the project at hand, without distractions. Created by Literature & Latte, the price is modest.

Grammarly is a cloud-based typing assistant which reviews spelling, grammar, punctuation, clarity and other mistakes in English texts. It can work in American, Canadian, British or Indian English. This program is AI-powered and can help correct errors. Use it as a guide; otherwise, it could change the meaning of a phrase. The basic version is free.

Canva is a popular online graphics program ideal for creating flyers, invitation cards and other promotional material. The basic version is free.

Affinity Publisher. InDesign is an 'industry standard' program for book design and layout. Challenging to learn, it is also rather expensive. If you do want to try laying out the pages of your book yourself, you could try Affinity Publisher. It costs much less than InDesign, but like its superior, it does also have a steep learning curve.

Mailchimp. You can send out a newsletter to a small group of addresses using a normal e-mail program. However, as the mailing list grows, your e-mail account may baulk at sending to many addresses simultaneously. Several good mass-mailing programs will help manage a list of recipients, handle address updates and format the newsletter to be received on a phone or screen. MailChimp is one of the most popular programs, and the basic version is free.

SOME USEFUL CONTACTS

The Alliance of Mission Researchers and Institutions

AMRI VISION: As members of the worldwide Church of Jesus Christ, joyfully affirming our commitment to the living God and his saving purposes through the Lord Jesus Christ, and empowered by the Holy Spirit, our vision is to establish and sustain a community of Christian institutions, networks and individuals engaged in mission research, facilitated through a secure online platform: https://www.amriconnect.net

The Society of Christian Scholars

The Society of Christian Scholars equips Christian academics to have a missional and redemptive influence for Christ among their students, colleagues, institutions and academic disciplines.
https://scshub.net
https://global-scholars.org/society-of-christian-scholars

Media Associates International

We equip and encourage Christian publishers and writers in hard places of the world to create excellent content that enriches the church and influences society. The power of the written word to transform lives and nourish people shines in the world's difficult places. Our work focuses on areas with few Christians and little publishing activity. We equip Christians to create life-changing books and articles in their heart languages through culturally relevant training tailored to meet specific local needs.
https://maiglobal.org

Regnum Books

Regnum Books is part of the Oxford Centre for Mission Studies (OCMS). Our books are the result of rigorous research concerned with the faithful witness of the church-in-mission, in all its rich diversity. Our books demonstrate authentic Christian engagement in the transformation of people and societies throughout the world and seek to bring the voices of academics and practitioners together in prophetic dialogue.
https://www.regnumbooks.net

Langham Publishing

Our publishing house is an initiative of Langham Partnership. Over several decades, Langham's three main programmes – Preaching, Literature and Scholars – have been equipping Christian leaders in the Majority World church and the work of Langham Publishing connects significantly with all three of these programmes. Today, across these four imprints, we publish around 50 books each year.

- **Langham Monographs** is an imprint focusing on PhD theses by Majority World scholars about theology and biblical studies, written with the scholar's context in mind.
- **Langham Preaching Resources** focuses on expository preaching and training and good quality, contextual books to support its ministry.
- **Langham Global Library** features a range of books on theology and biblical studies which address Majority World issues, by Majority World authors or Western authors who have been immersed in Majority World contexts.
- **HippoBooks** and its French-language counterpart **LivresHippo** have the specific focus of providing African perspectives on theology in the form of textbooks and other resources for students and faculty in theological education.

https://langhamliterature.org

APPENDIX: ADVICE ON MAKING MINIBOOKS FROM REGNUM BOOKS, BY DAVID CRANSTON

A thesis aims to prove to the academic community that you are capable of executing rigorous, robust research independently and making a significant, original contribution to the field. Therefore, your thesis is structured to demonstrate that, showing a depth of knowledge in your field and your ability to design and carry out a research protocol, gather appropriate data, analyse it carefully, present your findings and move from the concrete to the abstract in your conclusions.

But a minibook has a completely different remit and audience. A minibook is meant to give a more general audience (imagine you're writing for an intelligent 15-year-old) a simple, brief introduction to your topic. It's 15,000 words, readable in under 3 hours. You'll not only need to cut words; you'll need to simplify your ideas and arguments.

The aim is to simplify potentially complex ideas so that almost anyone can understand them. You are not trying to prove your academic credentials and grasp of long words but the practical, transformational benefit of what your scholarship has demonstrated. Ask yourself constantly:

- Does the reader need to understand this in order to understand the problems and solutions I have researched?
- What practical difference will this make to the reader?

Your book is a taster, and you'll have a list of further reading for those who are interested at the end.

One easy way to begin is to cut out 'fillers' – words that are put in that mean nothing and tighten your sentences. For example, in the phrase: 'was genuinely a complicated matter', the word 'genuinely' adds nothing. Taking a longer example:

Before:

> Prior to determining the case selection, I had to realise that getting the right sample was genuinely a complicated matter. I thought about this over a period of almost two years before I arrived precisely at these four cases. In 2007, before embarking on this research, I was in xxx talking with people about doing research concerning the xxx church, thinking that I could talk with all the main leaders in the entire country. I was interested to learn about the driving force behind their evangelism and their eagerness to establish new churches that appeared well embedded into their community. In xxx, the term for establishing churches among the evangelical Christians is *xxx*. Earlier, during the xx days, a church was called a *xx*, whereas today it is almost exclusively called a church. Following an internal dialogue with myself, I realised the hopelessness and absurdity of such a quest, and I was driven to think that I could interview all the founders of xxx churches before they were too old, as many of these primary sources were already between 70 and 90 years old. With the help of some local Christians in xxx, I started to make a list of key church founding people from the beginning of the xxx church epoch, which quickly grew long and was far from finished. As I reflected over the situation, the fascination of the – seemingly – well-inculturated xxx church has become more than any other issue a phenomenon that could lead me into further research. (256 words)

After:

> Before determining the case selection, I found that getting the right sample was complicated. In 2007, I was in xxx talking with people about the xxx church. I wanted to learn about their evangelism and their eagerness to establish new churches that were embedded into their community. Earlier, during the xx days, a church was called a *xx*, whereas today it is almost exclusively called a church. I realised the hopelessness of my initial task, but with the help of some

local Christians, I started to make a list of key people from the beginning of the xxx church epoch. My fascination with the xxx church could easily lead me into further research. (113 words)

BIBLIOGRAPHY

Adeney, Miriam. *Training Leaders to Write* (unpublished manuscript). Vancouver, Canada: Regent College, Vancouver, c1990.

DeMuth, Mary. *Fifteen Traits of Predatory Vanity Publishers*. Mary DeMuth Literary, https://www.marydemuth.com, 2022.

Derrick, Stephanie (editor). *Chasing Paper: Critical Reflections of Christian Books and Publishing*. Eugene, OR, USA: Cascade Books, 2021.

Dudley-Smith, Timothy. *John Stott: The Making of a Leader*. Leicester, UK: IVP, 1999.

Escobar, Samuel. *Mi peregrinaje con la palabra*. IFES Latin America (privately published), 1998.

Germano, William. *From Dissertation to Book*, second edition. Chicago, Illinois: University of Chicago Press, 2013.

Hsu, Al, 'Writing for a General Audience' (unpublished notes). InterVarsity Press, Downers Grove, Illinois, nd.

Hunter, James Davison. *To Change the World: The Irony, Tragedy, and Possibility of Christianity in the Late Modern World*. New York, USA: OUP, 2010.

Portwood-Stacer, Laura. *The Book Proposal Book: A Guide for Scholarly Authors*. Princeton, USA: Princeton University Press, 2021.

Thornbury, Walter. *Old and New London: A Narrative of its History, its People, and its Places*. London, UK: Cassell, 1898.

Veletsianos, George. *Social Media in Academia: Networked Scholars*. Abingdon, UK: Routledge, 2016.

Walls, Andrew. 'Christian Scholarship in Africa in the 21st Century.' *Transformation* 19/4, October 2002.

Walls, Andrew. 'Vulnerable, Interacting, Incarnate Faith.' *The Gospel and Our Culture Newsletter* 26, 1999.

Writers' Guild of Great Britain and the Society of Authors. *Is it a Steal? An Investigation Into 'Hybrid' / Paid-For Publishing Services*. London: Writers' Guild of Great Britain and the Society of Authors, 2022.

Writers' Guild of Great Britain. *Self-Publishing: A Step-by-Step Guide for Authors.* London: Writers' Guild of Great Britain, 2023.
Yancey, Philip. "Christian Publishing: Too Many Books & Too Few Classics?", *Christianity Today*, March 2, 1984.
Yancey, Philip. *Open Windows*, Thomas Nelson Inc, Nashville, Tennessee, 1985.
Zaid, Gabriel, in Jorge Herralde (ed). *Mito o realidad del Libro.* Bogotá, Colombia: CERLALC, 1994.

ACKNOWLEDGEMENTS

An idea for this small book has been in the back of my mind for some years but was brought into focus through conversations with Paul Bendor-Samuel, the Executive Director of OCMS (Oxford Centre for Mission Studies), with whom I have had a warm relationship for many years. My thanks also go to colleagues from MAI (Media Associates International), SPCK-IVP UK, IVP-USA and Langham Partnership International. Thanks to IVP-USA for permission to quote from two documents used to help potential authors think about repurposing dissertations / academic work for publication.

Amongst the many friends who have contributed ideas are Paul Bendor-Samuel, Professor David Cranston, John Maust, Ramon Rocha, Miriam Adeney, Milton Acosta, Angus Crichton, Sam Richardson, Ellen Hsu, Al Hsu, Rachel Hastings, Stephanie Derrick, David Baer, Alejandro Pimentel, Bethany McKinney Fox, Federico (Rico) Villanueva, Riad Kassis, Mark Arnold, Gretchen Abernathy, Christopher Hays, Monique Ingalls, Samuel Tedder, Darío López, Ruth Downie, Frances Mackenney-Jeffs, Ini Dorcas Dah, Adam Szumorek, Mark Carpenter, Colin MacPherson and, most importantly, my wife, Brenda Darke. Our thanks to Peter Barclay-Watt for the use of his house during a sabbatical period.

All errors and shortcomings are of course entirely my responsibility.

